AMBIVALENT MODERNS

AMBIVALENT MODERNS

Portraits of Japanese Cultural Identity

Lawrence Olson

Foreword
by
Ronald A. Morse

Rowman & Littlefield Publishers, Inc.

ROWMAN & LITTLEFIELD PUBLISHERS, INC.

Published in the United States of America
by Rowman & Littlefield Publishers, Inc.
8705 Bollman Place, Savage, Maryland 20763

British Cataloging in Publication Information Available

Library of Congress Cataloging-in-Publication Data

Olson, Lawrence, 1918–
Ambivalent moderns : portraits of Japanese cultural identity /
Lawrence Olson.
    p.   cm.
Includes index.
1. Japan—Intellectual life—1945–   I. Title.
DS822.5.O55   1992
952.04—dc20   92–874 CIP

ISBN 0–8476–7738–9 (alk. paper)
ISBN 0–8476–7739–7 (pbk. : alk. paper)

Printed in the United States of America

 ™ The paper used in this publication meets the minimum requirements of
American National Standard for Information Sciences—Permanence of
Paper for Printed Library Materials, ANSI Z39.48–1984.

In Memory of Catherine Porter

Contents

Foreword

I f you are tired of bleached economic analyses of Japan and yearn to peek into the hearts and minds of Japan's brightest modern thinkers, whose ideas still actively shape the debate about Japan's future, then this book is for you. If you appreciate good scholarship or enjoy fine writing, then you definitely want to read this volume.

As the reader might expect, outstanding books are produced by exceptional people and the author of this volume, Lawrence Olson, is a literary craftsman in the best sense of that tradition. He is one of those rare storytellers who can be captivated by the individuals he examines, but is never taken in by them. Armed with the tools of the Japanologist's trade—a thorough command of the language and original sources—Olson reaches into the careers of four Japanese contemporary thinkers and examines their ideas, feelings, hopes and fears. He makes complex ideas intelligible to the reader without reducing the intensity and significance of what the authors have to say.

Olson can accomplish this because he is fascinated with the topic and has followed the writings of prominent Japanese thinkers for decades. He first encountered the writings of the personalities examined here when he was in Japan in the 1950s and 1960s as the Japan representative for the American Universities Field Staff. Then it was his assignment to study,

understand and explain the issues he now writes about so
eloquently.

In the eyes of many, Olson has always been at his best as
biographer. In this volume he narrates the lives and ideas of
four of Japan's most interesting and important "progressive
men of culture" as he sometimes refers to them. Olson begins
his book with an essay on Etō Jun, one of Japan's most gifted
commentators and social critics and the person Olson knows
best on a personal basis. Etō, an old-fashioned nationalist, is a
key conservative figure committed to separating out the genuinely Japanese elements of modern Japan from the Western
influences.

While Etō takes on the West in his effort to rewrite Japanese
history, China scholar and journalist Takeuchi Yoshimi, the
focus of Olson's second essay, tries to relate Asia's revolutionary tradition to the Japanese experience. The third essay is
about an exciting populist writer and poet, Yoshimoto Takaaki,
who is preoccupied with writing about the place of the common man in Japan's recent history. Having explored the conservative and progressive dimensions of modern Japanese
thought, Olson turns in his final essay to an examination of the
life and writing of Tsurumi Shunsuke, the pragmatic, Ameri-
can-educated professor. Tsurumi has the most profound grasp
of American thought and philosophy and the most emotional
dislike of everything American.

There are numerous volumes covering Japan's political,
social and economic history, but there are few books like this
one that focus on the present Japanese intellectual scene of
the coffee houses and the essays in the monthly magazines.
The Japanese are avid readers of history, and for them Etō,
Takeuchi, Yoshimoto and Tsurumi, along with their followers
and the many others who appear on the pages of Olson's
analysis, define the context for Japanese thinking about World
War II, the postwar Occupation era, the 1960 U.S.-Japan
Security Treaty controversy, the implications of Japan's economic success and now the end of the Cold War and the
collapse of the Soviet Union.

There is no doubt that geography and language keep the

Japanese isolated from us and we from them. But with *Ambiv-alent Moderns* Olson shows us that despite this isolation, the Japanese in their quieter moments are struggling with the same timeless and universal questions that all moderns face. We sense this, but it is only when a dedicated scholar like Lawrence Olson takes on the task of explanation that we can indeed know it to be true. We are indebted to him for this.

Ronald A. Morse
Annapolis, Maryland
January 1992

Acknowledgments

The author is deeply grateful to the following who gave generous assistance: Etō Jun, Hashikawa Bunzō, Katō Shūichi, Miura Masashi, Walter B. Rideout, Hope Sage, Takeuchi Teruko, Lawrence Terry, Tsurumi Kazuko, Tsurumi Shunsuke, Yoshimoto Takaaki, and Charles W. Young.

The essay on Takeuchi Yoshimi was written in 1980 while the author was a Fellow of the Woodrow Wilson International Center for Scholars, Smithsonian Institution, Washington, D.C. Special thanks are due to Ronald Morse, former Secretary of the Asia Program at the Wilson Center, for friendly but searching criticism, and to Jan Yamamoto, for her assistance and constant encouragement in this as in other writing projects over a period of many years in Japan. Financial and other assistance was provided by the American Philosophical Society, the Return Jonathan Meigs Fund of Wesleyan University, and the International House of Japan. Publication of this volume was made possible by a grant from the Mitsubishi International Corporation.

The essays on Takeuchi Yoshimi and Yoshimoto Takaaki originally appeared in the *Journal of Japanese Studies,* University of Washington, Seattle; the former in Volume 7, Number 2 (Summer 1981), the latter in Volume 4, Number 2 (Summer 1978). Permission to reprint is gratefully acknowledged. The essays on Takeuchi and Etō Jun were circulated as Occasional Papers of the Wilson Center.

The author is indebted to Jeane N. Olson for invaluable assistance and advice.

Japanese word order for personal names has been followed, with surname before given name.

Introduction

The essays in this volume chart the careers and examine the writings of four contemporary Japanese intellectuals widely known in their own country. The essays are products first of all of the writer's interest in individual Japanese lives, an interest which began during the Second World War, grew during a decade of work in Japan in the 1950s and 1960s, and was sustained through research in written sources and numerous visits to the country in the 1970s and 1980s. Between 1955 and 1977, when the idea of the book first began to take shape, the writer met and talked with many Japanese intellectuals, men and women who dwelt more than most other Japanese on the discrepancy between what was and what might or should be in their society, and who took the whole of that society as the province of their writing and thinking. From among a wealth of persons with diverse attitudes and concerns, four have been studied who, I believe, illustrate the principal alternative paths or sources of nourishment through which postwar intellectuals sought to redefine their cultural identity and arrive at the meaning of Japanese nationality after defeat in the Pacific war. These paths were three: (1) the reevaluation of what was deemed usable in the Japanese past; (2) the study of Western modernization and the application of Western knowledge and ideas to Japanese circumstances; and (3) a vision of

Chinese revolutionary experience as a possible model for personal and/or national behavior.

It is a tribute to the diversity of postwar Japanese thinking about culture that any serious treatment of intellectual trends must take account of a wide variety of positions, attitudes and even visions; but underlying these essays is the writer's belief that the redefinition or reconstitution of the meaning of Japanese nationality, of cultural distinctiveness, with its implications of separateness and lack of connection with others, dominated the thinking of most intellectuals after the war, and was what gave their writings their basic force, feeling and unity, as well as their often noticeable narrowness of focus. Appropriating what they thought was needed from the outside world, they did not reach out to it with much warmth of spirit. This collection of essays offers in effect a retelling of early postwar Japanese history through nationalist intellectuals' eyes; their omissions are as valid an indication as their voiced themes of where they thought their concerns lay. The book is addressed to all those who are interested in modern Japan as well as Japan specialists and others concerned with the roles of intellectuals in developed societies. Beyond its biographical interest, it is hoped that it may provide useful material toward the writing of the intellectual history of Japan since World War II, to accompany the more numerous works in the political, social and economic history of the country.

Because the non-specialist reader has a right to expect that some framework within which to view this material will be provided, the writer offers the following brief introductory comments.

Japanese economic performance since the early 1950s is common knowledge; so is a context of overall stability in parliamentary politics. Postwar Japan has been correctly, if not comprehensively, perceived to be a conservative society driven by its felt need for commodity trade. Whether the resulting commercial policies have been aggressive or merely enterprising depends upon one's point of view, but most foreign observers have regarded cultural homogeneity, design-and-improve innovativeness, and a willingness to work hard and produce more as characteristic Japanese strengths in the economic sphere. Just so, many have remarked upon a certain reluctance to take prominent positions in international forums and a seeming preference for reactive foreign policies. Japan's hesitancy in the diplomatic area was not without reason. In the memory of the leadership generation, Japan utterly lost a major war, was occupied by the victorious side and forced to pay reparations to many of its Asian neighbors. Throughout much of the postwar era, when war with China and Russia had not yet been ended by a formal treaty of peace, when Japanese military capabilities were severely limited, and when the smallest economic initiative in Asia often ran the risk of exploitation in other lands for political advantage, it was not surprising that Japanese diplomatic initiatives were few and far between. (On Japanese activities in other Asian countries, see Lawrence Olson, *Japan in Postwar Asia,* New York, Praeger, 1970.)

From the late 1940s on Japan chose to become a close ally of the United States, with every conservative government affirming those ties. This policy was never seriously enough questioned by the Japanese people to cause them to vote the conservative establishment out of power; most people saw their country's interest as well as their own to lie in the American relationship and were willing to follow the government's economic rebuilding priorities under America's military protection. Not all, however, agreed with those policies. Indeed, for much of the postwar period, the government's pro-American alignment was a source of domestic political irritation, strife and disaffection.

Intellectuals, unsurprisingly, were especially disaffected. "Intellectual" is used here to refer not to the general educated classes, which in a country like Japan with mass public education since the 19th century would number in the millions, but to an intellectual elite, located in Tokyo, with much smaller contingents in Kyoto and other old national university centers, and consisting of professional writers, critics, journalists, and some but not all academics—a relatively small number of persons with nationwide visibility as commentators on the culture, persons accustomed to issue prescriptions for the solution of society's problems (and often presumptuous enough to try to set its moral and ethical direction). Among these self-conscious few, the pursuit of the meaning of Japaneseness had been a pressing activity ever since the 19th century; after 1945 it was set in the following general context.

First, Japan lost the war, and with defeat lost the certainties of an emperor-centered nationalism that turned out to be unequal to the goals and slogans it had set. Nearly all Japanese old enough to have views had supported their country's war on China and the West, at least outwardly. Their prostration afterward was, especially in the cities, complete. Nationalism was wholly, if temporarily, discredited and reduced to the level of the existential self. This led to considerable guilt and name-calling after the war, in which intellectuals, as preeminent users of the written and spoken word, participated. Controversies over war responsibility would have taken place even without the onset of the Cold War, but they were greatly sharpened by the anxieties it produced.

Secondly, the early postwar atmosphere of "liberation" and the Occupation's willingness to tolerate ideological diversity lasted for only a very short time. Even before the Supreme Command for the Allied Powers banned a general strike scheduled for February 1, 1947, the underlying nature of postwar political reality was becoming clearer. Conservatives in party groupings with links with prewar times won the first postwar election in April 1946. A weak conservative-socialist coalition held office for a few months in 1947–48 but from 1948 until the present, the leftist opposition stagnated at the level of a seemingly permanent minority. By 1950, many intellectuals who thought they had glimpsed the dawn of a new era in which "democracy" was equated with "liberation" or even with revolution were beginning to feel very disillusioned.

A good many of them were, of course, leftists or under some degree of leftwing influence. Marxism had been a strong influence in Japanese intellectual culture in the 1920s, before dissent was squelched. Marxist ideas again found wide acceptance after the war as an explanation for modern Japanese history as well as a program for future change. But by no means all intellectuals could be called Marxists. Many were romantic idealists who rejected Marxism's rigid ideology but were fearful of their own oppressive past and apprehensive of the outbreak of another war. Deeply distrustful of their own leaders and familiar with a tradition of oppression only from the right, they desired above all else non-involvement in world affairs, and adopted a touch-me-not attitude that was sometimes labelled "neutralism" or "pacifism" but that in any event was a pervasive characteristic of intellectual discourse in the whole postwar era. The lines were thus drawn in the late 1940s and early 1950s between a conservative government allied with the United States and with a majority of the people behind it, and an opposition supported largely by union leaders, intellectuals, and the young, but divided and scattered among ideological and personal factions.

These opposing forces, with their bitter prewar history, were further confirmed in their hatred and suspicion of each other by a series of events having to do with foreign relations. The Korean War brought an end to purges of the right; purgees were "depurged," and a "red purge" soon followed. In 1951 the Allies' decision to end the Occupation with a peace treaty of which neither communist China nor the Soviet Union was a signatory, and a military treaty leaving American bases on Japanese soil and the Ryūkyū Islands, a part of Japan for many years, under American jurisdiction, further embittered party politics and split the Socialist Party into left and right wings. Frustrated intellectuals organized demonstrations against American bases; other demonstrations kept alive memories of the atomic bombing of Hiroshima and Nagasaki. The conservative government's efforts to control these "fronts" and demonstrations and to preserve public tranquillity took the form of new police legislation, and moves began to rebuild the military forces. Predictably, these steps were followed by more demonstrations. In Tokyo a variety of intellectual journals, from the academic *Shisō* to the polemical *Sekai,* provided outlets for acrimonious criticism and debate over foreign policy. While the exact extent of their influence was impossible to quantify, what intellectuals wrote was widely read by the highly literate urban public; monthly magazines like *Chūō Kōron* had substantial circulations and carried serious, often controversial articles.

The era of postwar confrontation reached its climax in the winter and spring of 1959–60. Americans, who were either unaware of the extent of the intellectual disaffection or impatient with intellectuals as a group, tended to discount the importance of the Tokyo riots at that time and quickly forgot the headlines; however, Japanese intellectuals were profoundly shocked and moved to mass protests; they were briefly joined by a wide spectrum of urban citizens, and encouraged, even incited, by the mass media.

The issue revolved around whether Japan should, as the government sought, revise the Treaty of Mutual Security with the United States on its own initiative in order to gain certain political and diplomatic advantages. The original 1951 treaty had been widely perceived as having been forced on Japan as one price of the San Francisco Peace Treaty—another price being the recognition of Taiwan as the legal government of China—but intellectuals as well as large numbers of ordinary city people were badly frightened by what they took to be the possible consequences of Japan's taking the initiative to extend the treaty. For the Japanese government voluntarily to prolong the risk of involving the country in America's wars seemed intolerable to many.

Even had the government of the period been popular and handled the treaty issue with skill—and it had legitimate reasons of its own for seeking to revise the treaty—the whole matter would have been inflammatory. As it was, the government, widely regarded as the most reactionary after the war, chose to run roughshod over the opposition (itself admittedly obstructionist), forcing the revised treaty through the Diet under questionable circumstances and deepening the suspicions of the public. People of nearly every persuasion, from the YMCA leftward, opposed the new treaty in the streets and saw Prime Minister Kishi's "abuse" of his majority in the Lower House of the Diet as a sign of the peril in which Japan's parliamentary institutions stood.

The Security Treaty controversy brought many Tokyo intellectuals together in a common cause. As time passed and tempers cooled, spectacular economic performances, higher living standards, and a renewed search for "roots" dimmed memories of the crisis and reduced somewhat the sense of dependence on America; but intellectuals tended to look back to May 19 and June 6, 1960, days of mass protest and violence, much as they looked back to August 15, 1945, as a climactic moment in the history of modern Japan. By the late 1980s idealistic intellectuals had lost much of their prominence, their place taken in some measure by the brilliant and more technically "functional" managerial elite. But to the subjects of these four essays, whether or not they approved of the protests—and all but Etō did—May–June 1960 was the only time in the postwar period when to them true "liberation" might have seemed at hand, its spirit briefly realized in the street demonstrations, "fronts," "struggles," and "movements" of that turbulent spring in Tokyo.

Four intellectuals did not make a class or even a clique. Yet the fact that virtually nothing else had been written in English about these four, despite their undoubted fame in Japan, served to remind one of how isolated they were from us and we from them. Behind their wall of linguistic and psychological isolation, Tokyo intellectuals weighed and go on weighing endlessly the relative value of traditional Japanese culture, the virtues and faults of the "folk," the usefulness of foreign ideas. Power was not to be theirs, nor would they ever have to deal with the consequences of their romance with a "liberated" society. Yet in a period of anger, remorse and retribution in the years following the war, they and their dream of what Japan might stand for stirred many Japanese readers of their writings, who feared that the status quo ante bellum was dangerously near being reestablished. In their efforts to understand who they were after defeat, their arguments often proceeded from anti-imperialist premises. Yet their social criticism often was as much a product of visceral antagonism toward early postwar leaders tarred with the brush of "fascism" and militarism as it was an embrace of Marxism as an ideology or a system of historical explanation. These four men were first and foremost cultural nationalists, fearful of another war that would destroy what was left of their country. Most of them were bourgeois in their tastes and aspirations. But their ideas were in a fundamental sense conditioned by their wartime experiences, which had results that were the opposite of the liberal West's experiences. Knowledge of Japan's defeat, including its experience at Hiroshima and Nagasaki, reinforced their conviction of Japanese cultural uniqueness. What other people would have told a foreigner that he lacked sufficient *despair* to understand them?

L.O.

CHAPTER ONE

Intellectuals and the Search for Cultural Identity in Postwar Japan: On Etō Jun

For all Japanese old enough to remember, August 15, 1945 means the day when the Japanese emperor spoke to the nation by broadcast recording and brought his country's resistance in the Second World War to an end. Some who were too young to be in uniform that day heard his unfamiliar voice in war plants where they worked at making weapons or supplies. Others listened on ships, at base camps or in bivouacs, or crowded around radios in public places in the homeland, in China or elsewhere in Asia or the Pacific islands, wherever the broadcast was being relayed. Reactions varied with the age, station or temperament of the hearer. Most understood the message with its euphemistic language to be the equivalent of surrender. A few thought that it might be a veiled invitation to go on fighting to the last man. Some felt relief that they had been "liberated" at last. Others were angry at wartime leaders whom they held responsible for their personal betrayal and for Japan's national plight. Most were mutely accepting, but nearly all can still recall where they were on that day and at that hour. No other moment in modern Japanese history has carried quite the same emotional charge.

Among the millions who paused in their labors to listen on August 15 were an eleven-year-old boy and his grandmother in Kamakura. The boy's name was Etō Jun, and his grandmother, the daughter and widow of career officers in the Japanese navy, was to be the person most responsible for instilling in him a sense of the romance and achievement in Japan's modern past. But what he remembered most vividly about that day was her response on hearing the scratchy recording with its faint, elliptical message of capitulation: "How," she asked, "can he justify 'bearing the unbearable' to his ancestors, and especially to his grandfather, the emperor Meiji?" The pride as well as the sense of loss in that question were to remain with the boy for the rest of his life.[1]

This essay discusses the career and major writings of Etō Jun, who grew up in the 1940s and 1950s to be a prominent literary critic and writer on political and cultural subjects, versed in Western literature and culture but deeply sceptical of the uncritical acceptance of Western-style values or literary strategies for Japan; and who, in the 1960s and 1970s, increasingly stood for a tradition-conscious nationalism, as the more "progressive" intellectuals of the peace and anti-Security Treaty movements were losing their audience and the reading public was showing a renewed interest in the record of Japan's modern imperial past.

Finding in literary criticism a congenial vehicle for the expression of his conservative ideas about citizen, state and society, Etō took the artist's public duty versus the undeniable pleasures of escape from that duty as the theme of his early books on Natsume Sōseki and other modern Japanese writers, reflecting long-standing tensions in intellectual perceptions of Japanese society as well as in his own nature as an upper-middle-class youth of refined tastes growing up amid the confusions of Tokyo during and after the American Occupation. Two years at Princeton University in the early 1960s set going another kind of tension, between his distaste for both contemporary Japan and contemporary America and his growing awareness of the Japanese past, especially the Meiji past. In the late 1960s and 1970s he exhibited more and more irritation with America and Americans, who by the end of the period were being seen, not by Etō alone, to have become diminished in power and influence but still unconscionably manipulative of the Japanese for their own ends.

Throughout the thirty years after the San Francisco Peace Treaty Etō stood not against nor outside the Japanese political and literary "establishment," but in its mainstream. His books went through many editions, he was read by many thousands of people, and his views were listened to by a powerful few. By the 1980s, while he still clung to an image of himself as a literary critic, he had largely left criticism behind and was engaged on both sides of the Pacific as a commentator on Japan's relations with the United States, a lecturer to Japan Societies, a delegate to international conferences, a counselor of key politicians of the Liberal Democratic Party, even at one time a rumored candidate for a Cabinet position. His career was an instructive illustration of the frustrations as well as the gratifications inherent in the impulse of reaction against the pathologies of modernism in contemporary Japanese intellectual life.

I

Etō Jun (the pen name of Egashira Atsuo) was born on December 25, 1933, in the Ōkubo district of Tokyo, the eldest son of a middle-level Mitsui Bank employee. His family on both sides had navy roots. His paternal grandfather, Vice Admiral Egashira Yasutarō, was the son of a samurai, Egashira Yoshizō, who had been a little too old at the Meiji Restoration of 1868 to make the transition to the new order successfully. Etō himself felt his link to this ancestor:

> As long as Yoshizō is inside me and as long as countless Yoshizōs still dwell within present-day Japanese reality, I can never be an "individual" nor a simple "I."[2]

Yasutarō, by contrast, succeeded in his career, serving before his death in 1913 on the staff of Admiral (later Prime Minister)

Yamamoto Gonnohyōe and for a time as Chief of Staff of the
Sasebo naval base.

Yasutarō's wife, Etō's paternal grandmother, was the daughter of a samurai who opened a small academy in Kyūshū after
the Restoration but who, with a background in Dutch studies
and an interest in gunnery, was called up to help suppress the
Saga Rebellion in 1874 and later retired as a Lieutenant-
Commander in the Meiji navy. His great-grandson remarked
on his limitations:

> He lacked the concept of "society" that Fukuzawa Yukichi had
> . . . He knew the value of technology only through his own
> experience, and never realized that it was but one expression of
> "culture" . . . The image of education in [his] mind was not to
> offer new concepts but to follow old patterns.[3]

The grandmother, the strong figure of Etō's childhood memories, attended a girls' boarding school with Scots and English-
women teachers (but not missionaries) and imbibed some
information about the Victorian West; but to her, "modernization" was largely synonymous with her husband's career in
the new navy.

Etō's mother, daughter of a Rear Admiral from Aichi Prefecture, graduated from Japan Women's University, where her
principal teacher had studied at the University of Michigan
and Newnham College, Cambridge; she also heard lectures by
one of the teachers at Vassar College of the American novelist
Mary McCarthy; Etō would compare his mother's early decline with the fate of the women in McCarthy's *The Group*.[4]
His mother was considered "modern" by her classmates—the
word recurs as a measurement of idiosyncrasy in each generation—who thought that she might wish to find some work after
college; instead, she married at once: "For mother, marriage
meant accepting Japanese reality; for father's family, it meant
the arrival of 'modernity' and the beginning of unhappiness."[5]
His mother suffered for her "modern" inclinations: "Those
who become different by opening their hearts to the outside
must feel the terrible difficulty of being understood by those

who do not.''[6] And then there was her mother-in-law, who a generation earlier had been invited to visit Scotland by her teacher but had not been allowed by her father to go. ''Modern'' herself once, she now saw a new version of ''modernity'' in her daughter-in-law. Etō was too young to perceive their antagonism, which was to last until his mother's death of tuberculosis in 1937. She was 27, and Jun, her only child, was four.

Two years later Etō's father remarried and Jun entered primary school; he remembers sitting on his father's lap as he read in the newspaper of the spread of Japanese fighting in China.[7] But the boy's health was frail, and he was forced to stay home from school for long periods. Pining for his dead mother and dreaming of the exploits of his grandfather, the Vice Admiral, relayed to him by his grandmother, he began to read books very early, picking out the pronunciation of the characters with the aid of *furigana*. Some of the stories of Tanizaki Junichirō and a translated version of *The Count of Monte Cristo* were favorites. After the attack on Pearl Harbor the family was rusticated to Kamakura, where Etō entered a new school.[8] In 1944, with the war going from bad to worse, Etō's father built an addition onto the house and took in the grandmother, the Vice Admiral's widow. In May 1945 the family home in Ōkubo was burned down in an air raid and all their possessions were lost.

From Etō's references to his childhood one gets an impression of a physically weak youth, who was devastated by his mother's early death and given to reading and solitude. Music meant much to him, and he took violin lessons briefly; but on the whole his adolescence coincided with the worst period of postwar misery for the family of Meiji admirals. Too young perhaps to feel personally betrayed by Japan's wartime leaders, he was not too young to sense the family's decline.

Shortly after surrender they moved from Kamakura to more ordinary company housing in Hachiōji, in the western suburbs of Tokyo. Etō entered Tokyo #1 middle school and widened his reading: Russian and French novels in translation, Japanese poetry and criticism. In 1949 he had just decided to concentrate on French literature and had formed a small play-reading group among his classmates when a routine physical examination turned up tuberculosis. His father managed to find streptomycin on the black market, but Jun felt disheartened and left behind. After returning to school he began to write small prose pieces, translated a story by William Saroyan, liked to read Katherine Mansfield's writings and Conrad Aiken's familiar story of a boy's ambiguous withdrawal into madness, "Silent Snow, Secret Snow."[9] By this time he seems to have given up all thought of a conventional career in business or government service and to have conceived of writing as an alternative.

In 1953, aged 20, Etō passed the entrance examination for the literature department of Keiō University, but was once more stricken by tuberculosis and forced to withdraw for nearly a year. By late 1955 he had recovered sufficiently to be at work on his first book, a critical study of the novels of Natsume Sōseki, which came out in installments in the Keiō literary magazine, *Mita Bungaku,* during 1955 and was issued in book form in 1956 by a small Tokyo house, launching his critical career.[10] In the spring of 1957 he graduated from Keiō, married, and set up housekeeping in the suburb of Kichijōji.

II

Etō's writing life began as the Japanese economy commenced its prodigious postwar growth, and leaders and people began to turn to the task of constructing a new meaning for Japanese nationality at home and abroad. From the outset of his career he saw novelists as embedded in and reflecting the fabric of a specific political and social order. In this view, Sōseki had created a fictional world of high artistic value first of all because his books faithfully reflected the historical situation of certain Japanese individuals in the early part of the 20th century. Etō saw Sōseki as a "man of later Meiji," whose works were packed with the tension between society and the emerging self and mirrored Japanese social dilemmas at a particular stage in the process of modernization. To Etō, Sōseki was meaningless without his context:

> Before such men were writers, in a certain sense they had to be critics of their civilization. To write literature they could not ignore the problems that came before literature . . . In Japan there has been no society of citizens [of the town or city in the classic Western sense], no *shimin shakai*. Consequently, artists with a modern consciousness could hardly exist. While their bodies swam in the premodern mud, their minds chased the illusion of super-abstract "art" . . . The Japanese had no modern self in the Western sense, and so it was impossible to apply to Japan the rules and methods of the Western novel, which stands or falls by the existence of such a self.[11]

Japan's "poverty-stricken literary reality" might make impossible the "formation of novels by Western methods," but "that does not mean that Japanese reality itself is poverty-stricken":

> Being disloyal to the land that delimits one, or being insensitive to the influences that it gives to one, will not produce [literature] of true world quality . . . To be a world citizen one must first be a Japanese, an Englishman, or a Russian; just as Mark Twain rediscovered the American reality and was a true American, with achievements in a class with Columbus, so Sōseki discovered the reality of his own surroundings.[12]

Equating Sōseki's significance with his awareness of Japan's profound cultural differences from the West, Etō disparaged what he called "colonial literature" (*shokuminchi bungaku*) by writers of the dominant Naturalist school, who, he thought, had imported Western scepticism and anxiety and put their characters through anguish they read about in Western novels without necessarily understanding the different cultural basis for such responses to experience:

> They made Japanese their heroes and made them suffer torments they did not feel, and thus it was possible for the illusion to arise that our spiritual history had made the same progress as the West's.[13]

Etō realized well enough that loneliness and alienation, the cost of behaving in deviant "individualistic" ways in a society resistant to such behavior, was the main theme of Sōseki's best novels; in an apt phrase he located Sōseki's work at the point of "inflammation" (*ensho*) at the intersection of Japanese and Western cultures. In novel after novel written after his return from London in 1901, Sōseki had projected his disorientation in the modern world onto a variety of thinly disguised protagonists. But what interested Etō in these characters was not so much their personal difficulties or their neuroses as the insights their plight gave the reader into Japan's cultural situation as a whole. Thus, characters like Daisuke in *Sore Kara,* Ichirō in *Kōjin,* or Sensei in *Kokoro* were beached in a cultural sense. Deprived of the traditional crutch of dependence upon others, of access to indulgence from others for their acts in a new and lonely age, they could not go backward into an increasingly obsolete neo-Confucian universe nor forward into any "great free solitude, the choice of oneself in anguish."[14] All sought in one way or another to avoid the human connection, to shirk public duty and repudiate solidarity with others, but none succeeded in the attempt.

The novelist Mushanokōji Saneatsu thought that Sōseki had helped to enlighten and cultivate his readers by showing that the demands of the self took precedence over the claims of society. But Etō found Mushanokōji's interpretation mistaken: Sōseki could never put the impulses of the self above public duty; his characters had acquired only a sterile loneliness in return for their efforts at "self-liberation." And Etō boldly declared a lesson for himself in Sōseki's works:

I do not believe the myth that liberation is always filled with pleasure. Liberation always goes with illusion and a deep sense of loss. Sōseki felt this keenly. Because he was at last faced with the hard problem of how to deal with this huge anomaly of the self . . . The fact that he saw the revelation of the "I" as bad and painful, not good and beautiful, tells how deep was his sense of loss.[15]

Writing 40 years and two world wars after Sōseki's death, Etō believed the price his bereft heroes had had to pay for flaunting social conventions had deep relevance for postwar Japan. The self-society struggle was still going on. And he placed Sōseki in the pantheon of modern writers above such men as Shiga Naoya or Arishima Takeo, because in their concentration on the vagaries of the reflexive consciousness these writers had shunned the public function or role of literature and so were guilty of "immaturity." In their refusal to "socialize the I" they had to be labelled romantics. "What," wrote Etō, "is the 'I' that is nothing but 'I'?"[16] Or, as he put it elsewhere:

If the ultimate goal of Japanese "modernity" is to build an individual [kojin], then Sōseki took off from the problems that lay ahead in achieving that goal. Today, a hundred years after his birth, we have realized modernity in a sense, but the fact that Sōseki is more and more widely read . . . says that we have lost much that was precious in the process.[17]

Natsume Sōseki was a precocious performance for a 23-year-old and received praise from some important critics. Nakamura Mitsuo wrote that Etō "promises much . . . All his future critical activity will go toward fulfilling his promise."[18] Another critic wrote that Etō had betrayed a hatred of postwar Japanese reality and wished to find in Sōseki's writings the modern man he did not "crystallize" in "godless" postwar Japan.[19] Etō had indeed read a warning for the self in Sōseki's books; he had also sounded his particular nationalist note:

It may be that the value of art lies in transcending time and place . . . but those who create art must first of all live out fully the fate of their own time and place . . . The inflammation that arises between modern ideas and the realities of the premodern environment spreads through all the areas of our daily life. . . . [20]

Natsume Sōseki gave Etō access to publication in magazines, and in a series of essays in the literary journal, Bun-

gakukai, in 1957 and 1958 he elaborated upon the social function of the novel, lamenting that Japan had never produced a single novelist with the genius of China's Lu Xun, nor a single character as expressive of Japan's social truth as Lu's "Ah Q" had been of China's.[21] The energy of the Japanese people somehow had not found its way into literature. Instead, too many writers since the Meiji era had been seduced by a spurious "realism" which focused on descriptions of the writer's inner states or the trivia of his daily life. The true novelist could not abdicate his duties as a citizen. What exactly those duties were and what kind of society the writer was to be a citizen of, Etō did not explain, nor did he trouble to distinguish society very clearly from the state; but the drift of his thinking was clear enough. In Japan little was ever said about the civic responsibility of the writer; rather, literary criticism focused on the esthetic qualities of his work or his own quasi-magical abilities. This had resulted in a distorted set of artistic values:

> Should we not set forth on the adventure of creating a dynamic prose that can treat all of Japan's diverse reality in an inclusive way? Unless we do, we will not be able to give literary expression to our abundant national energy.[22]

In his next pair of books, produced between 1959 and 1961, Etō explored the writer's role in Japan's new mass society. His approach was as much moral as esthetic. What emerged from these early writings was a deeply serious concern for the reconstitution of an orderly society, and the controlling images in these books were images of responsibility, of action within rules or bounds, and of respect for the positive values of the past.

Thus in *Sakka wa Kōdō suru* (*The Writer Acts*), Etō pursued the matter of the writer's responsibility for social leadership into the realm of prose style. Words were tools in the service of a social purpose; they were "inseparable from human action." The writer should therefore "act" via his style to create the reality of his subjectively felt experience. As the swimmer escaped time by participating in the swimming match, so the creative writer's dynamic style contrasted with the static analyses of the social scientist, who was a mere spectator at the scene of his research.[23]

"Action" through the writing of images, not words as "things" or a "ready-made" (dekiagatta) actuality, was what Etō called for. He criticized the novelist Mishima Yukio for using words for their own sake: Mishima's language might be ornamental but he was preoccupied with "things"; and the imagination should be freed from "things." Likewise, the critic Kobayashi Hideo had

> made a metaphysic of the "negative style," the "style of non-action" which was the mainstream of modern Japanese literature. He alone *consciously* extended and developed the logic of that style. In a sense, he *acted out the logic of non-action.* His objective was to sanctify "things" [mono] by rejecting "reality" and legitimizing "stagnation."[24]

"Action" made possible an organic connection between the writer and society, gave the former a commitment and a reason for being. Great writers were great because of their dynamic imagery: "Words produce images, but when images are produced, words vanish, and we go beyond the trap [wana] of words that enclose our existence."[25] This to Etō was an act of true or selfless liberation: to establish one's style one must deny it, just as "to establish the self is to deny it, no matter what the modernizers say."[26] However, most modern Japanese novelists, he believed, had never ceased to cry "Look at me!" Wishing to "absolutize" themselves, they had retreated into self-glorification. "In modern Japanese literature, the individuality [kosei] that is able to act is exceedingly rare. All that exists are egos [jiga], stagnant, closed, inactive, [demanding] 'Look at my life!' " But first-rate literature came only from sympathy and common feeling for others, from the social nexus.[27]

Sakka wa Kōdō suru may have been heavily indebted to the vogue of Sartrean existentialism that swept Tokyo in the 1950s, but the book was noteworthy for its optimism. Though it had taken Japan far longer to create a modern literature than the technology of an industrial state, still the Japanese language, Etō thought, was alive, developing, and full of hope for the future.[28] This book was also interesting for its open political orientation. While Etō could never by any stretch of the imagination have been included in the company of Tokyo's band of leftwing "progressive men of culture," in the 1950s he was on good terms with a relatively wide variety of intellectuals in the Keiō University *bundan* and was attracted to some others who later took a very different course in Tokyo's intellectual wars.[29]

One upshot of *Sakka wa Kōdō suru* was a letter from the novelist Ōoka Shōhei, taking Etō politely to task for his negative assessment of the dean of living literary critics, Kobayashi Hideo. The fact that Ōoka had praised Etō's first book and helped to bring him to notice may have helped Etō to decide to take another, fuller look at Kobayashi.

Kobayashi Hideo was a long book filled with intimate details of the famous critic's life, his associates, friends and loves, as well as a minute, sometimes obscure, treatment of his literary ideas. It was in character for Etō to feel uncomfortable with Kobayashi's youthful writings, his infatuation with the French Symbolists, and his self-conscious attempts at self-discovery. Thus, in his early career Kobayashi had represented a "classic example of the abstractified city-dweller created by Japanese modernization," a mind filled with contradictions and paradoxes, whose instinctive strategy was to protect his "little absolutist nature in the midst of the relativistic urban environment of Taishō and Shōwa Japan."[30] Etō clearly was put off by Kobayashi's early desire to cut himself off from society as far as possible:

Why did Kobayashi, in the process of becoming a "pure and free individual," finally feel himself "distorted" and gnawed at by such a sharp sense of loss? Perhaps it was because his internality was gained at the expense of the literal obliteration of the other [*tasha*] . . . Man may be able to destroy the concept of society, but even afterward the other who makes him relative remains before his eyes. Just as there are inviolable secrets in his internality, the same secrets are in the other. But insofar as one does not premise the existence of the other, the dynamics of one's own self-awareness will not be established.[31]

However, as Kobayashi grew older he showed critical sympathies with which Etō had less reason to take issue, describing the older man as representative of a kind of Japanese nationalism in literature and approving his stand during the Second World War: retreatist, making no protest against the war, neither doubting victory nor expressing remorse in defeat. Moreover, Etō concurred in Kobayashi's high estimate of the novelist Kikuchi Kan, who had exalted the homely attributes of common sense and the performance of public duty. Kobayashi and Etō both found in Kikuchi's work qualities of solidarity and humaneness, "a world," as Etō put it, "in which alone there is true maturity."[32] And he quoted without dissent Kobayashi's description of Kikuchi as the "first writer to feel the importance of the social nature of literature not with his head but with his body, at the center of his individuality."[33] Thus Etō continued to warn of the penalties of not performing responsibly in society. Yet Kobayashi in his later work had moved away from a concern with the "modern" tensions of self and society, and like some others had gone back to celebrate more classical values: as Etō wrote, in Kobayashi's writings, "The more the core of the modern is approached, the more the spirit of primitive heresy appears."[34] And there was evidence that he approved of this, and that the later Kobayashi's writings about transience and death, his stress on the mysteries and the peace of nature as well as the asocial aspects of existence had considerable "charm" for Etō.[35] Likewise, he was moved by Kobayashi's view of history:

> . . . the outstanding men of every age have tried to overcome the age, and found their reason for living in so doing . . . Most modern views of history are theories of change, but could there not also be theories of unchanging history? . . . Man always fights against the same things.[36]

Kobayashi Hideo was a book of darker and more complex texture than *Sakka wa Kōdō suru* or even than *Natsume Sōseki*. Yet it was certainly unnecessary to call Etō a reactionary or worse—as a few did—because he allowed the minorkey vibrations in Kobayashi's later writing to speak to his own periodic need for the very "other-denying" internality, a private realm beyond the demands of society, which he had criticized in Kobayashi's early work.[37] In the last analysis what stood out in these first three books was Etō's insistence that novelists and novels in both style and substance serve a social purpose, which in the context of the 1950s to Etō meant helping imaginatively to redefine and reunify Japan's postwar mass society around stable, "orderly" values. Such values were in the young Etō's mind equated in a general way with the usable residue of "common sense" truths, which added together meant tradition and which implied the supremacy of the fabric of society over the individual's personal desires, his passion for such frivolous "esthetic" concerns as ornamental diction or a focus on the trivial details of the writer's daily life.

Thus by the late 1950s Etō, though still lacking in much experience of the world, already had shown a serious, indeed a rather solemn, concern for the literary critic's role in the processes of social and literary leadership. Stimulated by the reception of his work thus far, he withdrew from Keiō graduate school, collected a volume of his essays on writers, and set out to make his way as a freelance critic and commentator.

III

In 1960 Etō was 27, with several books to his credit and a growing reputation as a critic. So far he had won no prizes, but they would soon come. At this point something happened which moved his concern for his society out of the realm of literary interpretation into the harder light of political reality.

In 1958 the government of Prime Minister Nobusuke Kishi had managed to alarm a wide variety of Tokyo citizens by its heavy-handed attempts to revise the Police Duties Law to widen police powers of arrest and search. Since then the confrontation between the opposition and the regime had deepened; if Etō truly believed that writers should play public roles, it was time he became involved in some way.

For some time he had taken part in discussions with academic colleagues at Keiō on the troubling drift of domestic politics and foreign policy. In 1959 he published an article warning the government not to mistake all criticism for left-wing obstructionism; such blindness slighted the larger community, which wished only for genuine peace and freedom.[38] However, his own criticism of government was carefully measured. He seemed fearful lest official efforts to revise the U.S.-Japan Security Treaty to gain greater leverage vis-à-vis America might injure the national interest in some way, but he showed as much or more impatience with the rising street demonstrations against the treaty by labor unionists and students. Even those who knew no labor songs or slogans, he reminded his readers, could also have legitimate political demands; and he castigated the opposition for its transparently one-sided "neutralism": "All are not Buddhas in the USSR or devils in America."[39] He was uneasy with Kishi's high-handed political tactics, but disorder of whatever kind disturbed him most: the young mother who wrote to a newspaper that union sound-trucks were ruining her nerves excited his sympathy more than anti-government "struggles" then getting underway.

By the spring of 1960, as the crisis over the Security Treaty approached, Etō was active in a group of Keiō friends, classmates and others who called themselves the "Wakai Nihon no Kai" and who held at least one meeting with Miki Takeo and other leaders of the Liberal Democratic Party's anti-mainstream factions in an effort to cool the political temperature. It was Etō's first meeting with live politicians, and he came away sceptical that the weak leaders on the conservative "left" could ever form a front with the moderate socialists to stop the trend toward confrontation. Throughout the disturbances of late May and early June, his dismay at the behavior of the demonstrators matched his apprehension over the government's blunt tactics in the Diet.

The decisive moment for Etō in the impasse of May–June 1960 came on June 10, when he found himself at Haneda airport to cover for the *Mainichi Shimbun* the arrival of President Eisenhower's press secretary, James Hagerty, who had come to arrange for the President's proposed visit to Japan. Hagerty's plane put down to a mob welcome; he emerged from the plane "looking like a long-faced businessman" and had to be evacuated by helicopter to the American Embassy. As the student crowds milled around Hagerty's limousine and threatened to overturn it, Etō's "heart darkened," and he felt "despair at this huge amoeba," the mob.[40]

Predictably, the left opposition blamed the Hagerty episode on the police and rightist strong-arm squads, but Etō saw that this was not just: Communists and their sympathizers were clearly behind the provocation. He drew a lesson from the episode for Japan and for himself: what mattered most was a cold calculation of Japan's national interest in revising the treaty and remaining on friendly terms with the United States. By this reckoning, attacking Hagerty could hurt the country. But June 10 taught him a further, deeper lesson.

In an article published in November 1960 he bitterly attacked all those "idealistic" intellectuals who had interpreted Japan's defeat in World War II as "liberation" from militarism or "fascism" and who called upon the Japanese people to remain true to those feelings of release and opportunity which the "idealists" perceived had existed as of August 15, 1945, the day of the Emperor's broadcast of surrender. Etō himself had had no such feelings of liberation on that day. He never for a moment had accepted the idea that Japan's war on China and the West had been morally wrong, or based on a pernicious ideology of expansion that somehow had been dissolved by surrender, when the people had been given a supposedly new start with the more equitable institutions of the conquerors as their guide. For him such assumptions about Japan's war record were simply false, and grew out of the belief that the source of moral values lies in political devices. The basic reason for the outbreak of World War II was a conflict of economic interests, but our intellectuals look at the war only with an eye to deciding which side was morally justified. Japanese intellectuals have consistently refused to acknowledge the cold fact that politics and morality are incompatible, that one cannot obtain political power without getting his hands dirty.[41]

Excoriating the whole lot of "progressive" intellectuals, Etō offered an explanation for the way he thought they had rationalized Japan's defeat into victory:

Lying at the bottom of our intellectuals' extremely unrealistic thinking is their pride which was hurt during the war, when they realized that their country was undergoing its first defeat in history . . . Their wounded pride caused them to skirt reality and to plunge into a desperate attempt to create in their minds a make-believe world where Japan would never be defeated. As the end of the war approached and the signs indicating defeat became unmistakable, the intellectuals' visions of a victorious Japan became more and more fantastic . . . They simply let their own unstable emotions draw them further and further from reality. After defeat, they came out in passionate support of the new Constitution, which incorporated the principles of pacifism, democracy and internationalism. It is not so surprising that the same people who had so passionately supported the war effort should become absolute pacifists. These "progressive men of culture," although emotionally extremely radical, are nonetheless intellectually conservative and inflexible . . . In the long "war" which the intellectuals have been waging with reality, they have not had a single "victory."[42]

In contrast Etō praised those more flexible and public-spirited intellectual "realists" who had made no effort to sublimate their sufferings in surrender: "Those who really feel they want to participate in the workings of politics should give up their fanciful musings and morality and enter the fray as clearly defined political beings."[43] With such indictments Etō parted company with a number of his earlier friends. He had learned

that he would not protest to build an alternative politics. And
in the aftermath of the treaty "struggle" he grew more pessi-
mistic and withdrawn:

> I require only a politics that gives me freedom to live alone and
> die alone . . . Even if ties between men are possible, they live
> only by self-generating will and effort, and by no other power.
> To that extent all men are inwardly isolated. Who can flatter
> themselves that they know their husbands and wives com-
> pletely? Who can maintain that he has gone to the depths of the
> hearts of those who are dearest to him?[44]

His other writings following the Hagerty episode were
equally gloomy in tone. Each generation of writers thought it
was new; each rebelled; each was confronted with a "swamp
of illusions." He concluded that "my master is none but
myself,"[45] and that "it is wrong to say that all people of the
same generation have the same group experiences."[46] Such
ruminations alternated with more attacks on "progressive"
intellectuals. He was especially scornful of the group that
called itself the Institute of the Science of Thought (*Shisō no
Kagaku Kenkyūkai*), which in the 1950s and 1960s undertook
large-scale joint research projects on prewar and wartime
collaboration and other topics. Etō thought there was something indecently inconsiderate about their prying into other
people's motives and their readiness to use others for their
own ends. Such "social scientists" he believed were merely
impertinent: they wished to judge without being judged. But
"thought" could not be measured. It was not a "card in a
library or a patchwork of clothing sewn together."[47]

At this point in his career Etō professed to reject all systems
and ideologies of modernization, but he expressed admiration
for the work of the poet-critic Yoshimoto Takaaki, an intellectual who under leftist influence was in this period groping
toward some new formulation of Japanese nationalism that
would unite intellectuals with mass sentiment to produce a
sense of genuine cultural independence. The two men came
from very different backgrounds, but Etō praised Yoshimoto

for the honesty of his emotions, seeing in him a sincere searcher after the meaning of nationality in the fundamental feelings of the masses of the people whom he both distrusted and admired.[48] However, Etō could not adopt Yoshimoto's romantic "nihilism" for himself, and he had little to propose as a vision of the Japanese future except the rather conventional pursuit of the "national interest" and the careful protection of his personal privacy.

The Security Treaty crisis gave Etō some reputation outside classrooms and literary quarterlies. He now was identified more definitely as a "realist" intellectual with roots in the bourgeois mainstream of his society. As the final installments of his book on Kobayashi Hideo were being serialized in *Bungakukai,* he travelled briefly to West Germany to lecture at the invitation of the Bonn government. It was his first trip outside Japan. Soon after his return to Tokyo he was invited by the Rockefeller Foundation to visit the United States for a year.

IV

Etō and his wife arrived in Los Angeles on Labor Day weekend, 1962. That they both came was significant: they had no children and meant to experience America together. They knew almost nobody on the West Coast. The city was closed down for the holidays, and they had hardly arrived when Mrs. Etō was seized by a sudden and severe medical complaint. Etō had to find a hospital and get her to it quickly. Fortunately, her illness was not life-threatening, and after he had located a doctor and realized that she was in good hands, he began to feel better. Their experience was a good deal less traumatic than that of some others in foreign situations, but he dramatized it: in America only the fittest survive (*tekisha seizon*); he determined to be among the survivors, as he had when combatting tuberculosis as a child. He moved to a room near the hospital, ate tough steaks at the lunch counter of a neighborhood supermarket, and learned from a black taxi driver that the hospital was "predominantly Jewish." He was already making distinctions.⁴⁹ A few days later the Etōs arrived at Princeton University, where they were to spend most of the next two years.

As he wrote in his book on his American experiences, *Amerika to Watakushi* (*America and I*), Etō aspired at Princeton to get beyond "self-protective" attitudes of difference and to reach a sense of "liberation" in the awareness of differences; in other words, to emphasize the positive aspects of contact with another culture.⁵⁰ He brought important assets to the challenge of living in America and trying to learn from it. He had a gregarious personality, he spoke English, he was an observer with no fixed duties nor obligations to his government while abroad,* and he put his sharp critical powers to good use from day to day. He intended to avoid what he perceived as the chronic problems of Japanese visiting the United States: he would neither segregate himself with other Japanese entirely, nor ask endless questions in the manner of a newspaper reporter, nor associate only with Americans and take one long holiday. Yet like most people he was most comfortable standing in his own cultural territory, and he had hardly arrived before he was drawing national comparisons and making generalizations. For example, he conceived the notion that Japan had much in common with the American South; just as the Northern way of life had been forced upon the South, so the American way of life had been forced upon the Japanese. The United States had censured Japan for Nanking and Pearl Harbor much as the North had censured the South for slavery; and he compared the bitterness of the southerners' feelings toward the North with his own resentment toward America for the war and Occupation.⁵¹

From the first his critical curiosity was mixed with an edginess that he could never let go of, that he did not want to let go of. For example, he disparaged some American academics of his acquaintance who, he thought, believed that they

---

*He had originally intended to study F. Scott Fitzgerald but for whatever reason gave up the idea.

could assimilate to Japanese life simply because they spoke the language fluently; Japanese might be able to do this in America, as he was proving to himself, but the reverse was hardly possible, and those who tried wound up hating the Japanese.[52] Such points were easily scored; but while they may have shored up his sense of self-assurance, the need to score them at all was arguably a subtraction from his total experience. He obviously wanted to avoid falling into the "love-hate syndrome" he fancied some American students of Japan felt toward his country; but his traffic in such stereotypes soon had the effect of distancing him from American life and turning him back on his own foreignness, which was of course always available. This may have looked like wisdom to him but was still in some sense an escape: "I was accepted by Americans around me in proportion to my recovery of the self that had been hidden deep in my consciousness while I was in Tokyo."[53] No doubt this was true, but embracing "personal nationalism" ran the risk of narrowing his imaginative range.

Like most others visiting a foreign country for the first time Etō was busy in the beginning sorting out what he saw and coping with symptoms of disorientation. Princeton was like Kafka's castle; he could not connect with its concerns, and his feelings of attenuation were increased by the strange, somewhat dilapidated surroundings in which he and his wife started their domestic life. Friendly faculty members had helped them to find an apartment at 29 Wiggins Street, but it did not suit his needs, and about all he could say for their situation was that they were starting out as empty-handed as the early American settlers had done.[54]

If he had trouble getting beyond "self-protective" attitudes of difference, he did make some shrewd observations about American society in the last days of the Kennedy era and the start of the Johnson administration. He wrote a great deal about national differences; he seemed most comfortable at that level of generalization. For example, the Cuban missile crisis led him to conclude that while Americans might be deeply divided on race questions, their response to the Russians showed that "More than anything else, force carries

righteousness in America."⁵⁵ He decided that democracy was
first and foremost a symbol of their nationalism to Americans;
they could not abide Japanese or others who might appear
"anti-American" in the course of projecting their own conception of democracy.⁵⁶ He returned frequently to the theme of
the "tooth and claw" struggle in American life. Marriage came
in for some special criticism, for he could not condone the
fierce competitiveness of a society in which all social life was
conducted by the husband and wife as an isolated unit: "Indeed, American life is stark [*kibishii*]. They have nowhere to
flee if they distrust each other."⁵⁷ And he cited some obvious
references, Albee's *Who's Afraid of Virginia Woolf?* and Up-
dike's *Rabbit Run,* as particularly chilling treatments of marriage in postwar American writing.

Etō's first year at Princeton was a success in outward terms.
He made a favorable impression wherever he went, attended
and gave papers at scholarly conferences and was invited to
remain for another year, this time as a visiting lecturer in
Japanese literature. He had not come to terms with America
as a free individual making the "choice of himself in anguish."
His mind was bound by national stereotypes and by the bitter
memory of Japan's defeat, but he had come to feel more at
home about his own culture and his country's past: ancient
Japanese literature seemed closer to him in Princeton than in
Tokyo. Before taking up his new duties he made a quick trip
to Japan, where he was chagrined to discover that although
living abroad had made him more conscious of being a Japanese, he seemed like a foreigner to some Japanese at home:
the desk clerk of a Tokyo hotel mistook him for a Southeast
Asian, which led him to conclude sadly that "one doesn't live
abroad without paying a price."⁵⁸

His second year at Princeton was in some respects happier
than the first. He still felt resentments. He saw that Americans
had neither forgotten nor forgiven the Japanese for Pearl
Harbor, and he thought their personal kindness to him conde-
scending and hypocritical as long as they appeared to feel as
they did about the attack. He returned to the comparison
between Japan and the American South:

I feel that in a sense history has gone back to before 1941. Just as Edmund Wilson points out in the preface to *Patriotic Gore,* that the North's victory over the South did not spell ethical superiority, so in the Pacific War America's victory was no proof of American superiority. The Pacific war was a physical, biological collision between two expanding countries, like two primitive aquatic animals biting each other.[59]

Returning from a trip to New Orleans Etō found the people at Princeton cold. In the South he had discovered an irony he thought missing in New Jersey, an erotic confrontation of beauty and decay. He still saw America as a raw-edged place, and after President Kennedy's assassination in November 1963 he concluded that Americans had a "truly uncouth wildness."[60] But he was delighted to be elected a faculty fellow of the Woodrow Wilson Society, and from his Ivy League perch he pronounced declarations on American life:

Americans live by a daily struggle without mercy . . . I liked the merciless clarity engraved on the American system. At least it was based on a clear awareness of each person's bad intentions, and to that extent I could become aware of my own bad intentions.[61]

Or: "Loneliness is not an evil [in America] but a sign of strength."[62] Or, again:

The people of this country put up with hard work, make do with poor clothes and food, very seldom sing, dance, or get drunk. The police in America, the home of democracy, are far more severe than our "democratic police," and the federal government is far more powerful than Ikeda's cabinet with its "low posture." If one asks, is not this life hard and distasteful, one can only reply that at times it is. But in any case, this is what America is. It may bear some superficial resemblance to Japan, but it is a basically different kind of culture. It is also clearly different from Europe. It is not even "Western" but is an entirely new category [of culture].[63]

However, such observations, though telling, were overshadowed by the primary lesson which Etō felt he derived from his two years in America. This was that American intellectuals, whatever their other differences, felt a profound concern for what they took to be their country's national interest and wanted to serve a public purpose in a way he thought few Japanese intellectuals had done after the war. He wrote little about radical dissent in the United States during his stay, but he was deeply impressed by the civic values that he found to exist in Princeton society, deplored their absence in Japan, and lamented what he saw was the weakness of the postwar Japanese consciousness of the traditional state and its conventional role as the guardian of national unity. He blamed intellectual divisiveness in Japan on the "accumulation of estrangement and alienation between the state and the individual that has piled up in the half-century since the Russo-Japanese War"; and he warned of the consequences of such loss of devotion to the state: "Just as decadence stagnated at the bottom of prewar nationalism, so a deep decadence is hidden beneath the so-called universalism of the postwar era."[64]

Looking at Japan from Princeton Etō saw a spectre of dissolution, just as during the Hagerty episode he had seen a danger of mob chaos and disorder. He acknowledged the strong absorptive powers of American culture and came to feel that one part of himself "protruded" from Japanese society.[65] At one point he thought rather vaguely that if he stayed another year he might even become an American.[66] Yet after two years of American experience he felt moved to call upon the Japanese to reassert their own peculiar national interest and identify and prize their own cultural and esthetic values:

Esthetics are not necessarily universal. The fact that nobody today [in Japan] doubts the beauty of the Venus di Milo is simply because Japanese esthetic consciousness has been altered by imported education. I don't call that progress. There is a local or nativistic side to art. Instead of seeing the world in terms of a competition between two camps, democracy and communism, why not see it as many countries following organic impulses rather than men exemplifying ideologies? Why not see the Russians as acting out their dreams since the Czars of southward and eastward expansion, or China its memories of dominion since the Han and Tang? And who can deny that at the bottom of American policy in Asia there operates that strange passion to subjugate the open spaces of the West that the colonists were seized with from before the founding of the nation?[67]

Thus Etō learned to navigate American life at a certain depth, but in the last analysis he could not embrace a social ethos as cold and hard as America's was to him; much in American life actively repelled him. Individualism and unrestrained competitiveness as he observed them at work conjured up Confucian visions of disorder in his mind, no matter that the South's supposed "irony" seemed an appealing complication after a winter in New Jersey. Though he may have been transiently challenged by the freedom of American society, he drew back from it in the end; the lesson of Princeton for him was a reawakening of his Japaneseness, a complex of feelings rooted in his knowledge of his elitist origins and proceeding out of a deep distress at the postwar evolution of Japanese society. Thus if America spelled disorder and the absence of trails that he could recognize or want to follow for long, on his return to Tokyo he was shocked by the empty economism, the ethical desolation and conceptual nakedness of the place.[68] He seemed in danger of developing a distaste for both his possible homes; neither pleased him in the present, but he returned in 1964 attracted more than ever to the Japanese past and, at least transiently, more confident that that past possessed a permanent inner core of value:

What did we get when we received democracy from postwar America? We got responsible parliamentary government with the tripartite division of powers, and we got the abstract ideal of "liberty, equality, fraternity." Perhaps we got through the American notion of the "new" the results of a technical material civilization that had become "great." But we never got the "American way of life." Because, fortunately, Japanese society was not a vacuum, but was already fulfilled by its own "Japanese way of life." That was not inherently changed, in spite of land reform and changes in the laws . . . Whatever happens, the

Japanese must once again look into the "old" face of Japan with eyes unclouded by ideology and without being blinded by the violence of the changes all around them.[69]

V

Etō was only 31 when he returned to find Tokyo being transformed in the "economic miracle" that was fully underway. He was appalled at what he saw: "Standing at the foot of Benkei Bridge in Akasaka Mitsuke and gazing at the dried-up moat, I was seized with a profound yet hopeless feeling of distress and sadness."[70] The books he wrote in the next few years, years of enormous material progress for his country, articulated these wan feelings, even as he personally prospered and grew in reputation.

In *Seijuku to Sōshitsu (Maturity and Loss)*, while discussing several contemporary novels Etō deplored the postwar disintegration of patriarchal authority and the drive of today's Japanese women for more personal freedom, and he blamed such developments on the United States. Japan had entered the "church of democracy," and as one result the Japanese father-figure had been left in ruins, denied by both wives and children out of shame for defeat and their fear of being left behind in the scramble for the latest version of "modern" behavior.[71] Female characters in these novels now demanded independence and rejected the desire of their men to be permanently indulged:

> For Tokiko [in Kojima Nobuo's *Hōyō Kazoku*] the mother-role that is handed to her robs her of her youth. That can never be "paradise" to her. She wants the illusion of paradise not in the peace and repose of the "premodern" which her husband seeks, but in the liberation of the "modern." She wants to be young forever. Going to school had planted in him the hope of success but also the fear of being an "outcast" and of meeting strangers. But for Tokiko school had liberated her from the family and let her set forth, facing into the "modern." The "modern" was her youth . . . and her happiness.[72]

In these postwar novels mothers and wives were struggling to break the ties of "natural" relationships, to rise from the "mud" of traditional social relations and find "maturity" in "liberation." Etō knew that this movement, however slow in the aggregate, would not be reversed. Women in former generations had gone mad when forced to leave home in defeat. This generation suffered when it had to stay at home. But to their husbands, freedom from the wife-mother was too terrible to contemplate; it made them outcasts from themselves. They were unable to relate to any "other" outside the "natural" family. No god or nation any longer existed, and being free from a wife, even because of the wife's infidelity, was a fearful evil.[73] Etō also realized that the characters in these postwar novels were far richer materially than Sōseki's people had been, but he thought their culture as a whole was thinner. Sōseki's characters at least had known that there were fixed roles in society, whether or not they agreed to play them; but these postwar people had lost touch with traditional roles entirely.

What stood out in *Seijuku to Sōshitsu* was not so much Etō's perception of the Japanese cultural situation, as his pessimism and sense of loss, and his failure to see future solutions for social problems save by retreat into the now irretrievable certitudes of the Japanese past. Cut loose from the state and lacking religious belief, the characters in these recent novels were in a fundamental sense "disorderly." Etō's reaction to the social scene before him was dispirited:

> In modern Japanese society man can live neither for others nor for himself. To live for others, to take responsibility and try to rescue them, is to become bewildered. To live for oneself is to live without a god [*kami*], without reconciling to the world, and to fall into loneliness. So man cannot establish a "socialized I," and novelists, insofar as they start from the world in front of them and are faithful to it, must . . . depict characters unable either to hope or to despair.[74]

His response to contemporary social confusion was to call upon writers to act as if order and rules existed, and somehow to assume roles as "governors" (*chisha*) in their society:

> If we must unavoidably become individuals, if we are to be
> separated from the repose of those who protect us and each put
> in a position of exposure to the other [*tasha*], we can only
> become "governors" in order to supply the necessary minimum
> to continue our existence.[75]

Sōseki had written of the confused present against the memory
of a better time, when there were social forms and commit-
ments to be lived up to. Postwar novelists wrote flatly of a
present where all human connections had been broken, and
there was little or no consciousness that the past had been
better or even that it had been there. While it was not entirely
clear what he meant by such terms as "governors," Etō
appeared to be trying once more to stress the writer's social
responsibility:

> [Those who believed man to be naturally bad] feel that letting
> loose his nature invites anarchy and unhappiness. This is not the
> same thing as not believing in human nature. Rather . . . it means
> that when one tries to give some shape to chaos and disorder
> one will restrain "human nature" for the sake of protecting
> "humanity." Democracy entrusts to "governors" the job of
> harmonizing the thought of the majority. It is a system that
> connotes self-restraint. At the bottom of such a view of politics
> is a recognition that "nightwatchmen" must be ceaselessly at
> work, otherwise, the "governed" cannot live in security.[76]

In the mid-1960s Etō's writings sold well and he won more
prizes. However, books like *Seijuku to Sōshitsu* raised questions about the ultimate direction of his work. As the post-
Security Treaty generation, with its newfound prosperity and
its hedonism, came upon the scene, would he continue to
deepen an understanding of the ongoing problems of identity
in his society through literary criticism? Could he deal in
critical terms with what he took to be mindless self-indulgence
of much of urban society without giving way to a tendency,
strong in this book, to indulge in his own kind of cultural
despair? Etō himself was aware of these choices, as the above
quotations show, and as early as 1963 he insisted that he was

not advocating an exclusively nationalist literature, but simply that continuity with the past was essential in literature as in life.[77]

His visceral dislike for what he perceived to be the coarsening of postwar society increased after a visit in 1964 to the neighborhood of his family's prewar home in Ōkubo, which now reminded him of nothing so much as a hotspring resort full of cheap, one-night-stand hotels. Recalling that the grim meaning of the word "postwar" had first come home to him soon after surrender, when he fell for a confidence man's trick and was robbed of his father's "Boston bag," he lamented:

> In an era when material happiness becomes everything, to be stripped of material things is disgusting. Neither peace nor democracy rules in postwar Japan, but the pursuit of material happiness.[78]

He was conscious that his feelings were not shared by the great majority of his fellow countrymen, who in the rush to rebuild had wasted little time bemoaning their losses:

> I do not deny either that voices will be heard saying "the Meiji Japan that your grandfather made oppressed the people"; or that while my father was wearing a foreign necktie and riding a horse, others were being tortured by the special police. I do not deny that some will insist that while I may have lost much, the people [minshu] have gained much. I do not deny that many voices cry, "It serves you right. Wonderful! What is the state anyhow?"[79]

Yet he clung to his feelings of loss for the past, which had been good in spite of the evil it had led to; and he had only a "smile of pity" for those who called him a "turncoat" for his conservative views.

In the late 1960s and early 1970s Etō maintained his credentials and his self-image as a literary critic by writing a column of arts and literature commentary in the *Mainichi Shimbun*, where he often lamented the decline in the quality of Japanese novels and hence of the society which produced them.[80] However, the major portion of his time was occupied with research for large retrospective projects, such as a history of his family and biographies of literary and historical figures. He visited northern Kyūshū, saw the country of his father's samurai ancestors for the first time, and had trouble understanding the accents of the people he met. He travelled to London to collect material for a two-volume biography, *Sōseki to Sono Jidai* (*Sōseki and His Times*), which won the Kikuchi Kan Prize. He also wrote more about contemporary politics; in October 1968 he was in the United States to "cover" the presidential election in an article for the magazine, *Chūō Kōron*. Returning via Europe and the Middle East, he collected impressions which would be published as essays in magazines, which would in turn be collected in books with titles like *Common Sense, More Common Sense, Again Common Sense*. Like some other Japanese writers, he was becoming an industry. At the same time, he carefully protected his private life. During the day he might be incessantly before the public, but at night he liked to "forget the state, politics, society, the economy, and think about where I had come and where I might be going."[81]

While it did not attempt any further analysis of Sōseki's works, and in fact ended before his career as a novelist had begun, *Sōseki to Sono Jidai* was an able re-creation of the novelist's life, his friends and his milieu, and seized upon the essential themes in his nature. No doubt Etō felt some kinship with Sōseki. Both wanted loving mothers and neither had one; to both literature gave a sense of validity in a world in which they felt rejected. Sōseki went backward into the modern era; while Etō, though "modern" by every external standard, showed less and less patience with many of the effects of modernity. However, the comparison could not be forced. Etō had more self-assurance and far less creativeness than Sōseki; his personal life was by comparison with Sōseki's affluent, urbane, and "normal." Where Sōseki had seen English literature as something to "master" and through it to rise in the world and do credit to Japan, Etō, though obviously ambitious, was at once more facile and less pressured by public obligations. He professed to "protrude" from Japan in some way, whereas Sōseki would hardly have thought, even less have said in print, that staying another year abroad could have made him an Englishman. During his two years in London in 1900–01, Sōseki had seen images of hell in his fellow London rooming-house dwellers, a drained, careworn, working-class tableau.[82] Etō was merely amused and intrigued by his Princeton housemates.[83] Sōseki began to unravel in London; Etō turned his experiences in America into a best-seller.

VI

In 1971 Etō visited the United States again, addressed the Japan Society of New York on the state of Japanese-American relations, and wrote that America had become a world danger:

> I felt that Americans had no margin anymore and had grown smaller. They were angry at themselves. What would happen if they turned that anger outward onto Japan and the Japanese? Even diminished, America still has a great strength and is a great power politically and militarily. What if we are used as the scapegoat and outlet for this power?[84]

In 1973 he ventured into television with a script on the Meiji leadership (*Meiji no Gunzō*), which was broadcast over NHK. He was awarded another prize by the Japan Arts Council, and was received in audience by the emperor.

In 1974 he published the first of his popular biographies of naval figures, a study of the Tokugawa samurai, Katsu Awa (Kaishū), who played a significant role in the Restoration of 1868. This book sounded a somewhat broader note of nationalism than had been found in Etō's earlier writings. He approved of Kaishū's attempts to mediate the struggle between Bakufu and Court, to preserve Tokugawa income and control over Edo castle and build a new state without destroying the existing shogunate. These schemes, which Etō thought had been devoted to the higher goal of the preservation of the Japanese state, had ended in total failure, but Kaishū was one

of those "governors" whom Etō appeared to admire, a shrewd
nationalist who had worked with all his might to bring into
being a new regime with a minimum of Western dominance.[85]

Liberal-left historians of the Meiji era might criticize such
works as this one as well as Etō's later semi-fictional biography
of Admiral Yamamoto Gonnohyōe.[86] However, the appeal of
such books to readers was considerable, coinciding as they did
with the renewal of feelings of national pride and self-confidence during the period of the Tokyo Olympics, the centennial
of the Meiji Restoration, and the Osaka International Exposi-
tion. Security Treaty "struggles" now were a thing of the
receding past, and there was an impatient, even irritable note
when Etō wrote:

> A country must be independent . . . We may talk and talk about
> the West, and take what is good from there, but we must have
> something else, something we do not have. There is no man in
> Asia, so we copy the West. The West is huge in scale, it is lofty
> and grand. Because it stands perfect, all else naturally suc-
> cumbs. Japan is treated like a child, we are praised and chided.
> Can any good come of this?[87]

In the late 1970s Etō turned from biographies of such historical figures to an investigation of the American Occupation of
Japan, and in the autumn of 1979 he was awarded a fellowship
at the Woodrow Wilson International Center for Scholars in
Washington, D.C. to study literary censorship during the Occupation. Accompanied as before by his wife, he rented a
comfortable house in northwest Washington and commuted to
the McKeldin Library at the University of Maryland in College
Park and the National Records Center in Suitland, where
collections of original censored documents and other materials
are stored.

Etō's "Washington period" was a logical culmination of his
long preoccupation with the emotional and cultural distance
between Japan and the United States. His writings about the
Occupation represented another attempt to come to terms with
war and defeat on both the national and the personal level. In

the process he made some interesting discoveries and advanced his own interpretations of postwar events.

Much of his time in Washington was spent studying the history of a piece of writing by Yoshida Mitsuru, a former officer and survivor of the battleship *Yamato,* entitled *Senkan Yamato no Saigo—Tengo Sakusen ni okeru Gunkan Yamato no Sentō Keika (The Last of the Battleship Yamato—Battle Results of the Warship Yamato in the Tengo Operation).* Etō discovered that Yoshida's work had been refused publication by the Occupation's censors on three separate occasions, because, in the censor's words, it

> cannot fail to arouse in the minds of readers something like deep regret for the great battleship, and who can be sure that the warlike portion of the Japanese do not yearn after another war in which they may give another *Yamato* a better chance?[88]

In the face of the Occupation's Press Code, which reflected the determination of American policy in the days following Japan's surrender to suppress any lingering militaristic tendencies of the recent enemy, Yoshida had sought repeatedly through his own efforts and those of his friends and influential connections to have his composition published. Etō, who appeared to have rejected the notion that Japanese militarism or any other "evil" tendencies had caused the war with the West, deplored the injustice of the criteria applied by the censors:

> [Yoshida] was never satisfied with the action taken by the censors, because he was never convinced by the dichotomy between "democratic" America and "militaristic" Japan, an over-simplified picture of what had actually happened between the two countries imposed upon the occupied Japanese by the Occupation authorities. Why did he fight with all his "might and main" aboard the battleship *Yamato?* It was not because he was "militaristic" but because he simply wanted to fulfill his duty toward his country, just as his American counterparts aloft in their attacking bombers wanted to as well.[89]

What he learned of Occupation censorship brought out all
Etō's deep annoyance with the occupiers. The censors, he
insisted, had had no right to do what they had done; indeed,
by their own actions they may even have betrayed their envy
of Yoshida's own vivid participation in the *Yamato* disaster.[90]
Etō maintained that the censors had acted wrongly on two
counts: they had prevented Yoshida from completing his normal human process of mourning for his dead shipmates, and
they had condemned as "militaristic" a man whose only fault
had been to do his duty. Thus they had in effect cut him off
from a vital portion of his own and the Japanese past, both of
which had possessed undeniable elements of distinction, and
even glory.

Behind his writing on the *Yamato* case lay Etō's broader
contention that the Potsdam Declaration had constituted an
international agreement, according to whose terms Japan had
surrendered; that among those terms were clearly stated guarantees of freedom of speech, religion and thought, which
closely approximated the guarantees in the First Amendment
of the United States Constitution; and that therefore the censorship of books, magazines, newspapers, broadcasts, and the
like under the Occupation had been illegal in international law.
He further argued that the Occupation authorities were well
aware of these facts and that therefore they had enforced
official secrecy over the whole censorship operation in Japan,
even though it had been a matter of common knowledge there
that censorship existed.[91] Here was an interpretation of postwar events at variance with the often expressed Japanese view
of the Occupation as a period of "liberation" from militaristic
influences. The fact that Etō's arguments were based upon a
careful examination of documents in both Japanese and English and did not represent mere personal fulminations without
supporting evidence gave them additional weight. Other interpretations of the Potsdam Declaration and the Occupation's
policies were of course possible; but Etō's motives could
scarcely be condemned because he contested the views of
some Japanese more liberal than himself. Nor was it probably
just to accuse him of merely catering to the changed climate of

opinion of Japan in the later 1970s. What seemed more likely was that his own long-held conservative views had finally intersected the arc of public opinion which was itself moving in a more conservative direction.

In addition to these studies of censorship, while at the Wilson Center Etō also made his contribution to the long-drawn-out debate in Japan over the revision of the Constitution of 1946. In a book on the subject also written at least in part in Washington, he went over much of the same ground covered by American political scientists who long before had demonstrated what many had suspected: namely, that members of the Occupation staff had written much of Japan's new Constitution. Noting that censorship had imposed a prohibition on open discussion of the Constitution's origins, Etō maintained that ever since the end of the Occupation in 1952 a kind of "taboo" had continued to surround this subject, inhibiting a free exchange of views which might have made revision easier to achieve.[92]

Beyond his resentment over the way in which the Constitution had been drafted and made law by foreign command, Etō was particularly exercised by Article 9, in which Japan not only had renounced war as a "sovereign right of the nation" but had given up the "right of belligerency." Without defining precisely what he thought this phrase meant, he took Article 9 to constitute an unconscionable restriction on Japan's national sovereignty; he thus joined the camp of those whose advocacy of Constitutional revision for many years had been linked with an emotional revulsion against the Constitution's foreign "taint." This opened him to criticism from other "realists" who could not be accused of a left-wing defense of the Constitution:

> When Etō claims that a correct understanding of history has been obstructed to this day by the existence of a taboo "covering up and denying the fierce dissension between Japan and the United States over the Constitution's enactment," he is simply wrong. Many people support the Constitution while being fully aware of who actually wrote it. From their perspective, the claim

that the Constitution needs to be revised because it was imposed on Japan is totally unconvincing.[93]

The same writer argued that if by "right of belligerency" was meant the right to wage offensive war, then Japan was under the same constraints as other nations subscribing to the United Nations Charter; but if what was meant was the right of self-defense or the rights of a nation attacked and at war under international law, then these rights had not and could not be relinquished by any nation. He thought Etō exhibited "something close to a persecution complex" in his complaints and dismissed him as one of those people who "spout such arguments merely to vent their feelings of bitterness against the Occupation or to stir up a stimulating debate."[94]

Unless one appreciated the depth of Etō's feeling that Japan had been wronged by the American Occupation, one might wonder why, as late as 1980, he still openly called upon America to sanction Constitutional revision, something the Japanese government might have initiated at any time after 1952, had there been popular support for such a move. But to him the Occupation, which he tended to treat as a monolithic force, had not been a benign event but a travesty for his nation; and Etō had never purged himself of his suspicion that Americans, even in the 1980s, might still distrust the Japanese as they had done in the 1940s, and might therefore be guilty of hypocrisy when, for example, they put pressure on the Japanese government to increase military expenditures. To his rhetorical question, "If a stronger and less dependent Japan emerges, will they be able to endure it?"[95] his silent answer was "No." But it was also clear that he wanted such a stronger and less dependent Japan to come into being, even though he avoided advocating a more militant foreign policy:

> Japan must continue to develop peacefully, without becoming embroiled in any war arising in any part of the world, at least for the next twenty years . . . The recovery of the right of belligerency does not mean walking the road to war. It would not mean nuclear armament. It would only mean the regaining of sovereignty . . . [96]

VII

In his early books on Sōseki and other writers, Etō Jun insisted on the social responsibility of literature and those who practiced it: sympathy, solidarity, the affirmation of commonsense values, of "ordinary" life and its demands as well as its gratifications were what counted most to him in the novel, and even more than the novel; and he criticized what he took to be the asocial if not anti-social self-absorption of many modern Japanese writers of prose fiction. Yet, as was evident from his book on Kobayashi and elsewhere, along with the need to achieve "maturity" through responsible connection with others he also felt from time to time that history outside oneself was an illusion, felt the attraction of escape to a land where time did not run and where all things not present in workaday reality might be found.[97] As he grew older he became more aware of the tension between his inner and outer worlds; between duty and private pleasure; between the public nature of his role as a writer on politics, or the Occupation, or the Meiji past, and the world of his many volumes of essays on private themes—his pets, his eccentric daily routine, his fondness for black tea, for music, etc. Sometimes he thought admiringly of Rimbaud, whom Kobayashi had so admired and in whom, Etō believed, Self and Other had been mysteriously fused; and he acknowledged the "left-over" portion of consciousness, the region of intuitive being in which many Japanese had sought to satisfy their need for "nature" and the "natural" world. Indeed, it was clear that Etō wished to allow "nature" to usurp a portion of the territory of his experience, just as Sōseki had allowed himself to escape into the world of classical Chinese poetry and painting from time to time. There was thus a certain poignancy in Etō's search for some accommodation between the impulses of order, civic responsibility and national pride, and the demands of the private emotions. As he wrote in 1969, even the student protest movement in Japan could be seen as a manifestation of "nature," although it was a tragedy that it had to be expressed via the "tongue-tied vocabulary of development theory."[98]

But if he sought to keep an incontestable space for the
private sphere, with the onset of the Security Treaty crisis of
1960 and his travel abroad, the drift of his thinking grew ever
more public and political, and he became more preoccupied
with the past and how it could be made usable by the present
Japanese people as a whole. One saw this not only in the
changed subject matter of his writing but also in his ideas
about literature:

> Literary creation is a process in which you strive incessantly to
> readjust yourself to your own past. You achieve your identity
> only by undergoing this process of readjusting and reintegrating
> your own self with the organic whole of the culture to which you
> belong. In this process, you cannot possibly pick out one ele-
> ment of your heritage without also owning up to another: no
> facet of one's heritage can be suppressed. The past always
> comes to you as an organic, indivisible identity. It is no more,
> no less, than that.[99]

Etō was brought sharply into touch with his own past,
personal and national, during his two years at Princeton in
1962–64, at a time when the political turbulence of the previous
decade was being left behind and conventional nationalism was
once more becoming respectable. Another Japanese might
have been warped out of the mold of traditional attitudes about
nation and society by his foreign experiences, but Etō, with
his own brand of self-awareness, validated his Japaneseness
and fell back on his foreignness in America, while in the
background of his conservative reactions to America there
stood the spectacle of Japan's own ugly modernity—rootless,
as he thought, undignified, lost, as he saw himself, amid the
gritty traffic of Akasaka Mitsuke. Returning to Tokyo at a time
when his fellow countrymen were fully launched on their
unprecedented economic odyssey, Etō wrote a series of biographical works set in the era of national power and profitable
wars at the end of the last century, when the Japanese realm
could be imagined to have rivalled Victoria's in brilliance,
personal relationships were (in retrospect) predictable and

sure, and writers had only begun to lose their sense of solidarity with the polity and to feel afflicted by the general modern anxiety. Reacting strongly against post-Occupation social reality, he refused, for example, to regard the liberation of women in Japanese society after World War II as a good, and instead looked back with fondness to a supposedly more ordered and elegant, even if a less equitable, world. Surely there must have been a sense of full circle having been reached in his mind when for his critical accomplishments he was invited to at least one audience with the same emperor whose voice he had heard on the surrender broadcast as an eleven-year-old child.

One Japanese observer thought that by moving away from serious literary criticism and toward more popular and polemical works, Etō had increased his isolation from his contemporaries.[100] Yet his popular biographies, although they marked a kind of declining spiral from the originality of his early work, did communicate a real sense of pleasure in the writing, and there could be no question of his satisfaction with his discoveries regarding Occupation censorship or the Constitution of 1946, and the opportunities these afforded him for using some Americans as whipping-boys upon whom to vent feelings of indignation and hurt pride.

However, there was more to Etō Jun's career than a mere conservative reaction to personal or national misfortune, more than creating or exploiting a transitory mood of nostalgia for Meiji. His young manhood had coincided with the dismantling of the absolutist state which his own forebears had helped to bring into being. As a beneficiary as well as a victim of the postwar disorder he professed to detest, Etō learned a great deal about America, and hence about himself and his own country, during his two years at Princeton, and unlike some of his countrymen, was able to become a relatively whole-hearted participant in a living Western society, not just to stare at it as an outsider and see an alien civilization staring back. Coming to believe that most Americans, whatever their other differences, were profoundly concerned for their country, he became concerned for his own. This led him to conclude that

democracy, as defined by the American Occupation, had not
been internalized by the Japanese, and should not be; this in
turn led him to realize that what he perceived as a loss of
Japanese pride and sense of identity had begun long before
World War II and was connected with the whole process of
modernization since the mid-19th century. Even as he yearned
for Meiji in many ways, he saw that it was then that things had
begun to go wrong.

Where his rather disconsolate line of thinking would lead
him was unclear; he was still not yet 50 as this article was
written. Some of his Japanese critics had long identified him
with the "new right" which had emerged after the Occupation;
others thought they saw in his later works evidences of prewar-
type "old right" tendencies. But Etō tended to slip away from
such attempts to label him. His Meiji period itself hovered
between the imaginary and the real. Like some others he
wished to use the past imaginatively to supplement and enrich
the empty, disorderly present. His heroes were the successes,
not the failures, of that past: Ōkubo Toshimichi, the prosaic
nation builder, inspired him more than did Saigō Takamori, the
brilliant failure. Etō's outlook also contained a strong element
of status-consciousness: "I felt about the Meiji state as though
in a certain sense my grandfather had fashioned it."[101] Indeed,
the conventional state appeared to be vital for him to give an
external sanction to his self; but he was probably too self-
aware ever to hold extreme views. His visceral recoil from the
mob at the time of the Security Treaty crisis had, in the words
of his biographer, demonstrated that "fanaticism was farthest
from his nature."[102]

To some of his more progressive critics Etō's thinking about
the 1946 Constitution and the Occupation was bound to seem
dubious. Some deplored what they took to be his tendency to
equate sovereignty with state (*kokka*) power rather than to
accept the sovereignty of the people as stated in the Constitution. Some also noted that while the Occupation had practiced
censorship in its eagerness to suppress whatever it imagined
might be militaristic tendencies, at the same time some writers
had flourished after the war, and their views of censorship

would naturally differ from Etō's. To a good many people wartime and prewar treatment of writers had been more severe than anything the Occupation had been guilty of. Such critics also noted that the question of Constitutional revision had been brought up only infrequently by both government and people in the generation and more since the war, and that opinion polls revealed that the people for the most part thought the Constitution a good thing and supported it.[103]

Few Japanese presented a more complex mixture than Etō Jun of fastidious literary privatism, old-fashioned nationalist sentiment, and distaste for the fractured modern spirit. In the final analysis his world-view was heavily conditioned by conventional, Western-oriented attitudes of material ambition and achievement. Almost nowhere did he write of the rest of Asia or show much interest in other Asians; his mind, like the minds of his Meiji protagonists, literary or otherwise, was focused on how and whether Japan measured up to the West—a point of view that may still have been pervasive in the generation before 1980 but that promised to become less fruitful in the years ahead, when most of the West's technical lessons, at least, had long since been learned. Some might suppose that a program for the Japanese cultural future was urgently needed, but for those seeking such a program Etō offered little beyond a rather static vision of a society in which fathers behaved, at least to themselves, as if they had not lost their influence and authority, and writers as if they were somehow playing public parts in the national drama. Meanwhile, like most other contemporary intellectuals, Etō's own private life was a mélange of sophisticated tastes and activities, a life spent teaching and writing, reading Western literature from Agatha Christie to William Faulkner and Japanese literature from Mishima to the *Manyōshū,* listening to Mozart and Chopin on the stereo, offering his views on Western political developments to Japanese politicians privately and on television, travelling and living comfortably in the West, and walking his cocker spaniel in the hills around Karuizawa.

1984

CHAPTER TWO

Takeuchi Yoshimi and the Vision of a Protest Society in Japan

On May 21, 1960, two days after the U.S.-Japan Security Treaty had been passed by the Lower House of the Japanese Diet in circumstances of questionable legality, with the police called in to remove forcibly Socialist members who had blocked access to the rostrum in the House Chamber, Takeuchi Yoshimi (1910–1977), one of the most prominent members of the Tokyo intellectual community and a widely respected authority on modern Chinese literature, resigned his professorship at the Tokyo Municipal University and sent the following notice to his friends:

> When I began my employment as a professor I took an oath to the effect that I would respect and protect the Constitution as a public official. Since May 20, I believe that parliamentary government, which was one of the objectives of the Constitution, has been lost. Those responsible for the loss of function of the Diet, the highest organ of state power, are none other than the Speaker of the House and the Prime Minister, the most senior of public officials. In view of their disregard for the Constitution, for me to continue in my post as a professor is to disobey my oath of office. It is also against my conscience as an educator.

Consequently, I have decided to resign. This decision is mine alone, taken without anyone else's interference. This step was not encouraged by others, and I have no intention of encouraging others to do likewise. I have the ability to support myself by writing, and I chose this step as my way of protest, after mature consideration.[1]

Whatever the logic of his action—two hundred people wrote him letters about it, two-thirds approving, one-third disagreeing, some threateningly[2]—Takeuchi's public gesture attracted wide attention. This was not the first such gesture of his career, but it came at a moment when Japanese emotions over foreign policy differences and Takeuchi's own dissatisfaction with the status quo both had reached their highest pitch of postwar intensity.

This essay explores Takeuchi's career and major writings in an effort to show how the ideal of personal and national regeneration, derived especially from the work of the Chinese writer Lu Xun, took root in one noted intellectual's mind before and during the Second World War, and how he clung to his vision of Chinese mass protest against foreign and domestic exploitation as a model for Japanese society and personality throughout the postwar period, even into the 1970s.

Takeuchi's case illustrates better than most what it means to work throughout one's life with all one's sympathy, imagination and skill, as well as with one's biases, misconceptions and lapses of insight, in short, with all one's strengths and short-comings, for an ideal out of joint with the times. To sustain such a course took strong character. For just as most of Japan's political and commercial leaders faced toward the West in the period after 1945, so most intellectuals were preoccupied with various aspects of Western knowledge and the fashioning of that knowledge to Japanese use. In the immediate aftermath of war and defeat, relatively few professional writers and critics—intellectuals who took the whole of their society and its problems as their subject—focused their attention upon China. A burden of guilt toward that country remained here and there, but the study of modern China was not fashionable, especially in the universities. There were, of course, older reasons for this than war, defeat and occupation. In the traditional academic view, history to be respectable had to be remote in time; Chinese studies in Japan had long been governed by an approach that stressed textual exegesis and the accumulation of facts; attempts at synthesis or the injection of a point of view were frowned upon.[3] Before 1941 such attitudes, along with the greater prestige of Western studies, kept many university students away from Chinese subjects. One who did not stay away but who endured noted:

> As a young man I got a hopelessly pessimistic impression of Sinology and Oriental history. . . . Sinologists of the time . . . held to a nihilistic opinion that any attempt at interpretation was a source of fallacy. Someone said that historical positivism is the ruin of scholarship; I felt I was lost right in the middle of the ruin.[4]

After the war the older tradition of Sinology (*kangaku*) persisted, but by the time of the takeover of the mainland by the Communists in 1949 a number of more progressive Japanese specialists on the modern period were active on the fringes of or outside academic circles, in study groups or societies of non-academic or semi-academic intellectuals, often equipped with their own journals, more or less radical ideologically and given to a more frankly political point of view. Where many scholars in the older tradition had approached China convinced of the superiority of Western civilization and its rule of reason, in the postwar era fewer had confidence in a standardized model of the West as the non-West's universal goal; many were reluctant to look for Asia's future in the West's past, believing rather that "prewar Orientalists failed to perceive the dynamic developments in China which were indicative of an achievement beyond the modern West."[5] Acceptance of communist China as a qualitatively different kind of civilization peopled by "new men" implied a criticism of the whole idea of modernization conceived primarily as a quantifiable process through which all societies undertaking it perforce must pass.

In the early 1950s, as the American Occupation drew to a close and a new debate on Japan's cultural identity and world role got underway, it was not difficult to detect nationalistic overtones in the writings of some of these students of the new China. For if China was in truth different in essence from the West and indeed superior to it, it behooved Japan in its own interest to make amends that were long overdue and somehow to draw nearer to the Chinese model. In other words, some Japanese intellectuals called for Japan to purge itself of colonial attitudes toward Asia and for a politics of mass protest in order to achieve a new society.

One of the best known of these intellectuals writing on modern China was Takeuchi Yoshimi. What were the springs of action that led him at the peak of a long critical career to the center of the movement against the Security Treaty? Why did China, rather than the West, or the Japanese past, absorb him during a lifetime of critical activity? What was his contribution to the intellectual discourse of his times, and why was his work regarded by a number of influential Japanese themselves as in a real sense crucial to an understanding of those times?

I

Takeuchi Yoshimi, an eldest son, was born in 1910 in Usudamachi, Nagano Prefecture and brought up in Tokyo. His father's family had produced Shintō priests for generations before the Meiji Restoration in 1868, but by Takeuchi's childhood the family was in decline. His father left a government clerkship to engage in business ventures in the Ikebukuro section of Tokyo, eventually becoming involved in the world of entertainment and the demi-monde: the *karyūkai*, or "flower and willow world."[6] As a child Takeuchi was ashamed of his family's lack of money. He was never close to his father; of his mother, who died when he was fourteen, he wrote nothing; later, his stepmother, who seems to have been a semi-professional *samisen* performer, was said to lack the capacity to understand his literary inclinations.[7] Other recollections of his early life were stereotyped but consistent with an unhappy childhood. Perhaps the first of his dramatic personal gestures came in 1923, when he took everything he had written up to that time to Inokashira Park and burned it.

He attended Kojimachi Primary and Tokyo Municipal #1 Middle School (now Hibiya High). For higher school he went to Osaka, where he had relatives, probably to get away from home.[8] There he took literature courses, read some German philosophy—Nietzsche, Stirner, Kant—finding the latter incomprehensible. He disliked German, never learned French, and was not attracted by Western writers or by Japanese writers under Western influence: the Shirakaba group did not appeal to him, but he loved Turgenev and read *Fathers and Sons* in the Constance Garnett translation when he was eighteen. Of his three years in Osaka very little is known. He was picked up once by the police and held overnight on suspicion of Communist Party activity, but no prosecution followed.[9]

In April 1931 Takeuchi entered the Chinese literature department at Tokyo Imperial University. Later he liked to explain that he chose this course because the entrance examinations for it were easier than for law or economics, and also because he felt empathy with the weak and demeaned.[10] He may also have selected Chinese because he did not feel liberally endowed with the more conventional abilities (*shūsai*) necessary for success.[11] But whatever the true reasons, the decision to study Chinese was to determine the whole direction of his life.

He started with the modern colloquial language, without any background in the classics, and read for the most part works written during and after the May 4th Movement and the "literary revolution" of the early 1920s. Many years later he wrote that to him the true enemy of creativity had always been *kangaku* or traditional Chinese studies.[12] At Tōdai he was in a tiny minority of students: of thirty-four in his graduating class in Chinese studies, he alone specialized in modern literature; in the class after him, of twenty-nine such graduates none had this specialty. His senior paper, on the writer Yu Dafu, was said to have been only the second written at Tōdai on a contemporary Chinese literary subject. (The first was on Lu Xun.)[13]

In the summer of 1932 Takeuchi travelled to Manchuria and north China for two months on a Japanese Foreign Ministry travel grant. This trip changed his life. In Tokyo he had been a lazy, unmotivated student, drinking half the night and sleeping most of the day. Now he fell in love with the Chinese scene: "The moment I went I felt this was home. What mattered now was not whether doing Chinese literature would be interesting or not; I simply felt I could do nothing else."[14] His first attempts to get close to ordinary Chinese were touching, their results fairly predictable: "What can I add to this man?" he wondered about his rickshaw puller, and quickly realized that as a foreigner with very imperfect spoken Chinese, the answer was little or nothing.[15]

Written a few months after the Japanese invasion of Manchuria, his account of this initial encounter with China had an incongruous but engaging naiveté. The impact of the trip was definitive, and gave him something with which to compare Japan for the first time. On returning to Tokyo, he and a small number of friends set about forming the first of many study groups, the Chinese Literature Study Society (*Chūgoku Bungaku Kenkyūkai,* or CLSS), which met regularly from late 1934 and in early 1935 began issuing a small, twelve-page mimeographed bulletin, *Chūgoku Bungaku Geppō,* a vehicle in which they might publish translations of current Chinese writing, their own essays and news of mainland literary happenings. Takeuchi was clearly the leader of the group.

In his senior year Takeuchi's reading included works by such contemporary Chinese writers as Lao She, Mao Dun, Ding Ling, Dian Han, Lu Xun and others, as well as *Das Kapital* in Japanese translation and such famous Japanese Marxist compilations as the *Nihon Shihonshugi Hattatsushi Kōza* (*Lectures in the History of the Development of Japanese Capitalism*) and the writings of the Rōnōha Marxist leader, Yamakawa Hitoshi, whom he liked for his clear, jargon-free style.[16] Graduating from the university in 1934, he wanted above all else to return to China, and in order to get there would have been glad of a job in the South Manchurian Railroad Research Bureau. But with little except literature on his record, he had no choice but to devote full time to the magazine.

From the outset he and his friends, including Takeda Taijun, later to become famous as a novelist, regarded China as a deeply nationalistic society whose process of breaking with its past was insufficiently understood by their fellow Japanese. This attitude, gained from early reading and contact with Chinese writers in Tokyo in the 1930s, and ratified by his visit to the mainland in 1932, was to be fundamental to his entire career as an intellectual criticizing his society.[17] At the same time, while he looked upon his government's combative policies toward China and the West alike with misgivings, he showed no more disposition than other Japanese to demonstrate against those policies. Indeed, in the absence of much information about the mainland from leftist sources, then in process of being suppressed in Japan, he was not averse to joining the East Asia Society (*Tōakai*), which counted among its leaders the noted propagandist Ōkawa Shūmei, who was to appear in 1945 as a defendant at the Tokyo war crimes tribunal but was judged unfit for trial. As Takeuchi himself later wrote:

The periodical, *New Asia,* came out at this time, largely through Ōkawa's insistence. Compared with the earlier *East Asia,* it was less academic and more in the nature of an education journal, and included many maps. The area covered was not just East Asia but the whole Asian region. It was something new, a precursor of the idea of the Greater East Asia Coprosperity Sphere, and I read the magazine with great pleasure.[18]

In the fall of 1936 Takeuchi received another grant from the Foreign Ministry, this time from Boxer Indemnity Funds, to study in China. His departure was delayed by the outbreak of the Marco Polo Bridge incident in July, but he finally arrived in Beijing that winter. He lived with a Chinese family and started on a course of reading, but things had changed since his 1932 visit. Japanese troops now occupied the city, nearly all Chinese writers had gone south, and those who remained in the city kept to themselves. Beijing seemed culturally asleep, with most Chinese-returned students in the front lines as interpreters. He still wanted to "connect" with China and thought it could be done, and he dreamed of reaching an understanding of the mentality of Chinese soldiers through a study of individual writers and their works. But he had mixed feelings about the actual scene before him. The China he loved was being ruined. During this rather melancholy time he first read Sun Yat-sen's *San Min Zhu I,* and his imagination was fired by Sun's nationalistic vision.[19] Yet he could not help being glad that he was a Japanese, felt swept up in events, and spent much time drinking in bars and helping to spread what he called "Tokyo coffee-house culture" to Beijing.[20]

Writing in 1941, Takeuchi transmitted some of the foreboding he had felt during his two-year stay in China:

> When was it? At some point a light went out inside me. It had been a dim light, to be sure, but when it shone there was at least some standard for action. Now, though I wake at midnight, it does not shine. Who put it out, did I? I know not, but the reason has to do with my trip to China. When I went the light shone, now it does not. My diary for that period is a void. . . .[21]

In late 1939 he returned to Tokyo. He was by now a "China-hand" but still lacked regular employment. He was at loose ends; his father had died during his absence and the family had moved from its old home in Shiba to a strange new address in Meguro. In early 1940 he took a job in the Islamic Research Center, a government-sponsored agency engaged in accumulating information about Moslems in China and elsewhere in Asia. This gave him a chance to return to the mainland briefly in 1942, when he travelled around northwest China and wrote reports on conditions; but he does not appear to have had any real interest in Islam. In this period also he came across Edgar Snow's *Red Star Over China* and read it in English, but the book's stress on the young Mao Zedong was not immediately meaningful to him; later he indicated that the Comintern's influence in China had blinded him to Mao's importance before 1945: "Japanese were unready to understand Snow with their hearts during the war. And they only understood the united front after their own defeat."[22]

When the Japanese attacked Pearl Harbor, Takeuchi issued a statement fully supporting the war:

> To speak frankly, we had difficulty agreeing at once with the China Incident. We were assailed by doubt. We loved China, and that love supported our lives. As China matured, we matured, and we believed in that maturity. When the China Incident occurred, that belief crumbled. Cruel reality disregarded our existence. . . . We grew paralyzed and drifted. . . . We ignored the so-called holy war, without shame for our stupidity. Was not our Japan, hiding behind the euphemisms of East Asian upbuilding, actually oppressing the weak? But now, Japan does not fear the strong. The deeds of the autumn frost [Pearl Harbor] prove that. Is there any happiness beyond this for us as one people? All is now clear; our doubts are dissolved. . . . The true significance of spreading the new order in East Asia and liberating its peoples penetrates our bones and shapes our determination. . . . We love Japan first, and neighboring countries after Japan.[23]

Commenting on this statement in 1972, Takeuchi defended the sincerity of his patriotic feelings:

> It was mistaken as a political judgment, mistaken from head to tail; but the ideas it contained were not themselves mistaken; however they may be judged a crime by others, I would have no choice but to go to hell carrying those ideas.[24]

After the war with the West began, publishing the magazine became more and more difficult. Paper rationing went into effect in December 1942, and the police put the magazine on a list of suspect journals and frequently visited its offices. In early 1943, when he voluntarily suspended its publication, Takeuchi justified the decision in the following terms:

The Greater East Asia war may be called the rewriting of the
history of the world. I deeply believe this. It means the denial of
modernity, of modern culture, and out of this denial, to build for
oneself a new world and new culture. . . . Modern culture must
be denied, because it is the projection of Europe onto ourselves.
Thus we must in a sense deny ourselves. For the creation of
history, the world must be produced from within. . . .[25]

In December 1943 he was finally called up and sent to central
China in a railway guard unit. He remained there as a private
soldier until August 1945 and then served as an interpreter for
nearly a year after defeat and demobilization.

II

"We need have no moral doubts about routing the invader
from East Asia. The enemy must be thrown out with one
stroke of the sword."[26] How far Takeuchi made such statements from an impulse of self-preservation and how far he
genuinely subscribed to them it would be useless to try to
guess. Obviously he shared in the chauvinistic enthusiasm of
the immediate post-Pearl Harbor period. Yet he had been
depressed ever since his return from China by the discrepancy
between Japan's slogans and its policy realities there. He was
disgusted with the seamier side of the Japanese presence in
China; he deplored the wartime narcotics trade; stories of
Japanese selling drugged candies to Chinese schoolchildren
appalled him. Though he wrote of these things only after
defeat, he was conscious of them during the war and they
weighed on his conscience.[27] Moreover, *Chūgoku Bungaku*
(the name was shortened about 1940) had been his main
interest ever since 1935, the mainstay of his intellectual life.
By January 1942 the CLSS had grown to around one thousand
members, and stopping the magazine was not easy for him.[28]

In this complicated state of mind, exhilarated and depressed
at the same time, as he waited to be called up in 1943, Takeuchi
wrote his first important work, *Rojin* (*Lu Xun*), a two-hundred-

page book which was to be published in December 1944. Later he recalled that he had written the book in a driven spirit, at a time when his life was being threatened by the war and when he wanted to leave some testament behind.[29]

Lu Xun's brief, bitter chronicles of the humiliations and abuses of village Chinese in the early years of the Republican era justly made him the most famous modern Chinese writer, in China as well as in the world.* Lu showed the youthful Takeuchi a vision of what literature could and should be: socially concerned, deeply nationalistic, close to the bone of daily life, expressing human values in hard, specific situations, and implying the necessity for protest and revolution, especially a revolution in the spirit to produce "new" men and women for a new Chinese age. Lu's impact, like China's, on Takeuchi was emotional and direct; he saw Lu as not so much a political writer seeking, like Liang Qichao, to use literature for activist purposes, as a brooding, often despondent and sardonic figure, a looming figure of despair whose writings amounted to acts of atonement for China's terrible plight under the burden of its own warlords as well as Western and Japanese imperialist pressure. Lu's sad characters—the Madman, Ah Q, Gong Yiji, the Passerby who must forge ahead toward "a place without landlords . . . without cages and expulsion . . . a place without smiles on the face and hypocritical tears,"[30] expressed a quality of heroic endurance that Lu had found in some of his Russian models, notably Gogol; but they were also slavish, tragic *Chinese* figures, devoured literally and figuratively by the family system, landlords and bureaucracy.

Much of Takeuchi's treatment of Lu was taken up with trying to classify him, to separate out his political and literary qualities: *Rojin* is the book of a young man not yet very sure of himself. Why he found himself in Lu Xun is not entirely clear, but seems to have been an accident of his education and his travels as much as anything else; but for those circumstances, he might equally well have specialized in French or English literature. But what he found in Lu basically were the

---

*1881–1936. Cf. *Selected Stories of Lu Xun,* New York, W.W. Norton, 1977.

values necessary for revolution from within and below, a call
for self-renewal and self-respect, Lu's terrible, heart-gripping
admonition to his readers to "save the children" for the age to
come. In the midst of a Japanese war of extermination against
China, Takeuchi grasped in Lu Xun a protean vision of independence for the wretched of the Chinese earth. This vision
warmed his thoughts in a cold time and fed his emotional
yearning for some kind of solidarity (*rentaikan*) with ordinary
Chinese. Nothing he had read in Western literature had struck
him with the same power or immediacy. He had seen these
characters of Lu's or others like them on China's streets, and
at an impressionable age. (He never met Lu himself.) All that
was needed now to complete the circle of his feelings was to
apply Lu's values, his guilt for China's plight and his expiation
of that guilt through writing, to Takeuchi's own country in the
context of defeat, foreign occupation and the Cold War. All
that was really needed to root Takeuchi's mature view of man
was to ask the passionate question: "Why was there nobody
like Lu Xun in Japan?"[31]

Lu Xun's writings defined Takeuchi's basic imaginative experience and gave him his postwar subject. His search for an
understanding of Lu's message of the need for mass reconstruction has been compared in its honesty and intensity with
the search of the French intellectual Simone Weil for identification with French factory workers in the 1930s, or Jean
Genet's search for the world of "the blacks." Each to some
extent became what he or she wrote about.[32] In Takeuchi's
case, however, there was a special, "Asian" effect. "A man
like Lu Xun," he wrote after the war, "could not have been
born in a European society, one that has no limits on progress,
or in Japan, where the illusion of progress is believed."[33] To
Takeuchi, Lu showed that the "special conditions" in which
the Chinese were placed were more Asian than universal, and
left little room for the contemplation of universal values.
Obviously ideology entered in here: for Takeuchi, foreign
imperialism was largely to blame for China's plight; but whatever the balance between the dialectic and the viscera, Takeuchi in his mature career tended to focus on the Asian world

and to fall sometimes into a rather crude East-versus-West pattern of thought and feeling. Lu's characters may have had qualities of universal victims, but it was their victimization as Chinese, not their generality as human beings, that Takeuchi felt most keenly.

Takeuchi's book on Lu Xun implied, though it nowhere stated, that Japan's whole modern effort in China had been based upon an inadequate grasp of Chinese national aspirations. His writings in the three decades to come would call again and again for a society based not upon "Western-style" but upon "Chinese-style" values, a "protest society" in a Japan with weak traditions of mass protest:

> From Lu Xun's protest I gained a clue to understanding my own feelings. My own thinking about protest came afterward. If I am asked what protest is, all I can answer is, something like what is in Lu Xun. And that there is no such thing, or very little of it, in Japan.[34]

III

Takeuchi read the Potsdam Declaration of July 26, 1945 in a Hankou newspaper: "It was a distant event that had nothing to do with me." A few days later, he heard the Emperor's broadcast of surrender on the unit's only radio, but like many others was unable to tell whether it was a signal to give up or to go on fighting to the last man—he thought probably the latter. He felt a mixture of joy, hatred and despair, and a "feeling of infinite sadness, like a wilderness where I had never set foot before." He had foreseen another outcome: America would invade Japan, the leaders would split into war and peace factions, and a revolution would sweep the country. He would join the partisans in the back country. Obviously this romantic scenario never came to pass.[35] He returned to Japan in July 1946 and began to write in order to eat, translating from Chinese and soon publishing his first essays.

His early writings projected a vision of revolutionary nationalism derived from Lu Xun and Sun Yat-sen directly onto postwar Japanese society. Although superficially the times may have seemed to him congenial to ideas of liberation and protest, underlying political realities in Japan could hardly have been more unsuited to the goals he advocated. Instead of moving to unite with Asian nationalism, most Japanese accepted the necessity for a more gradualist political future in close alliance, political and economic, if not psychological, with the United States. Most people deeply wanted to forget the war and to concentrate the blame for defeat as far as possible on the military. But to Takeuchi the past was totally unresolved. The rain of war had settled nothing but had left great pools of guilt all over the landscape, guilt for defeat, for a bankrupt Japanese "destiny," guilt toward a China misused and little understood. Whatever the merits of the Allied Occupation—and he was not beyond realizing the advantages of a greater personal freedom for himself—to him Japanese modernization had failed once and for all, and should have no second chance. Until the past had been atoned for and Japanese mistakes in China admitted, no postwar leaders could be trusted.

With this overall mental stance Takeuchi struck forward into the postwar intellectual scene. He sounded his characteristic note early, in a June 1948 article on "Lu Xun and Japanese Literature" ("Rojin to Nihon Bungaku"), portraying Lu as a folk hero who sought to remake the self from within; by contrast, the Japanese had aimed to escape from colonialism by appropriating Western devices and becoming a colonial power themselves. Later in 1948 he wrote several long articles in which the comparison with China was extended, always to his own country's disadvantage. He attacked the vulgar competitiveness of the Japanese, their compulsion to chase after the West, their "slave mentality" (*dorei konjō*); he deplored the absence of a "spirit of savage protest" such as had appeared in modern Russia and China, and of what he called a "negative possibility" or "chance for denial" (*hitei no kiki*) in modern Japanese history, where a tragic dimension seemed lacking and suffering had not been understood.[36] He thought the Japanese lacked maturity; they sought only to forget the past and rush blindly at the future.[37] (Many years later he was to see this habit at work in the joint negotiations for a peace treaty with Beijing, where the Chinese delegation wanted to reach a general agreement which acknowledged that small differences remained, while the Japanese side tried to wipe the slate clean, pretending that the past had never existed and denying any differences whatever. He could not have foreseen that by the late 1970s the Japanese government would be eagerly ignoring political differences with China for the sake of contracts for oil exploration and other economic opportunities.)

In these attacks on his own people and their characteristics in a period of abject defeat there was more than a little self-hatred.[38] The corollary of this feeling was disgust with the upshot of the war and a deep-running stream of ethnic nationalism (*minzokushugi*), very evident in "Chinese and Japanese Modernity" ("Chūgoku no Kindai to Nihon no Kindai"), of November 1948, a piece that greatly enhanced his reputation and that was reprinted in the October 1964 issue of the magazine *Chūō Kōron,* along with seventeen other "articles that shaped postwar Japan."

Here Takeuchi saw Asia in stark terms as the passive object of Europe's irresistible expansion, a veritable creation of Europe's dynamic outreach. With its faith in rationality, Europe was positively frightful (*osoroshii*) to him. In China, Mao Zedong's communists were living out Lu Xun's moral scenarios and producing "new men" to take over the country; meanwhile, in Japan there was no protest, no struggle. Aside from a few ineffectual poets, such as Takuboku, modern Japanese literature had been uniformly degenerate (*daraku shita*). While the Chinese had shown themselves capable of self-renewal (*kaishin*), the Japanese could only flipflop from one superficial position to another (*tenkō*). Copying from the soulless, scientific West, living in sin without remorse for its record in Asia: this was the grimly moralistic picture of Japan that Takeuchi evoked. Above all else, the Japanese were slaves, with slaves' diligence. And what was worse, they were not even aware of their slavery.[39]

Such romanticizing of the Chinese revolution might not have gone down with most Japanese, but it struck a sympathetic note among some idealistic intellectuals searching in the post-war ruins for a self-respecting and ideologically congenial alternative to the bankrupt emperor-centered nationalism of the past.[40] Here, clearly, was another nay-sayer to the new age of onward and upward secular capitalist growth. Where other writers took as their texts other talismanic phrases, like community (*kyōdōtai*) or individual autonomy (*shutaisei*), Takeuchi appropriated Lu Xun's "China" as the symbol of an energizing purpose, a paradigm of protest and struggle essential to his self-esteem, as to his country's, in a period of national and personal humiliation. Like Yoshimoto Takaaki's "people," Takeuchi's "China" was no less real because it was probably unattainable; instead, it served a vitally affirming purpose as an object of aspiration and an abstract good.[41]

"Chinese and Japanese Modernity" brought Takeuchi to the notice of a wider audience and his writings were soon in demand in a variety of magazines and newspapers. In April 1950 he directed an outburst at the Japan Communist Party for its obvious subservience to the Comintern.[42] In September 1950 he attacked the San Francisco Peace Treaty, signed without Chinese or Soviet agreement, and called for a broad but non-violent "people's movement" against the treaty.[43] In the same month he published a fiery article, "Modernism and Problems of Ethnic Nationalism" ("Kindaishugi to Minzoku no Mondai"), accusing Japanese intellectuals of ignoring the "folk." Social revolution in Japan, he argued, had never occurred because the values and goals of the "folk" had never become the engine that alone could move it forward to realization. Rather, the statist values of the emperor-centered elite had been imposed upon the people from the top down; instead of fueling revolution, as happened in China, nationalist sentiment in Japan had been channelled into capitalist modernization, which in turn led to imperialism and a disastrous war.

Pursuing this argument, he insisted that a new mass move-

ment was necessary, complete with a new literature of the
people, to somehow connect nationalism not with a class, nor
with a mystical Japanese "spirit" that had failed once before,
nor with Western-style "universalism" but with "permanent
protest and liberation," Chinese-style. Criticizing the custom-
ary division of Japanese fiction into "high" and "low" writing,
works of esthetic excellence by acknowledged stylistic masters
such as Tanizaki or Kawabata, and potboilers for the mass
market, he called for a people's literature (*kokumin bungaku*)
that would spring from communal sentiment. It is hard to know
just what he had in mind; presumably, something analogous to
Lu Xun's genre pieces from the Chinese villages, or perhaps
Synge's Irish fishermen, or Brecht's Mother Courage. At any
rate, he rhapsodized about the idea of the "mass base" that
he now saw only too clearly to have been the key to Mao
Zedong's success in China. Like Lu Xun, Mao had gained all
by losing all; where Lu had turned his despair at the apathy
and self-justifying hypocrisy of his fellow-Chinese into marvel-
ously penetrating vignettes of China's social sickness and need
for renewal, Mao had turned the weakness of the Jingganshan
period into the power of 1949. To Takeuchi, Mao's base in the
peasantry was an internal country, a country of the mind as
well as a geographical entity, a place where both a revolution
in social relationships and an overturning of individual values
could take place.[44] Only out of such a base could a true
people's literature ever come.

As he wrote more and became involved in more controversies, Takeuchi began to draw critical fire. One critic accused
him of an "existentialist" interpretation of the Chinese revolution.[45] Another claimed that in his attack on Japan's modern
history he merely replaced Europe with China as the utopia:
his conception was as dependent as that of the Westernizers
on a foreign model. Moreover, to this critic it was obvious that
Takeuchi, for whatever reason, saw all "modern" progress as
distortion and insisted on praising in China what most other
Japanese saw as backward. He quite ignored the liberal democratic tendencies existing in Japan ever since the late 19th
century, however weak and spasmodic they might have been;

surely, the trend toward truly democratic "liberation" was not reprehensible merely because it had not envisaged an uprising of the "folk." Moreover, Takeuchi had firmly closed his eyes to all the efforts that had been made after the war to improve relations with mainland China, including the beginnings of new research on that country, new friendship organizations, trade, and the like. He focused on Japanese guilt; but the Beijing regime distinguished between the Japanese people and their government, and did not (or so it was alleged) retain hatred of the former. Takeuchi claimed that Chinese communist morality was rooted in folk tradition; but merely declaring that "the Chinese revolution reveals the fundamental strength residing in the folk" was really not very helpful in understanding modern China.

There were further dangers in this focus on the "folk." The same critic noted that Takeuchi had used John Dewey's writings on China to argue that the Chinese were more capable of revolution than the Japanese. But Dewey took moral values to be the main cause of social change in China and saw American-style democracy emerging there under America's paternalistic protection. Dewey neglected the "objective" factors: modernization of production facilities, growth of people's capital, and emergence of a working class in China after World War I. The rise of Chinese communism, this critic thought, could not have been predicted from Dewey's observations. In the same way, Takeuchi's tendency to idealize the "folk" contained within it the seeds of a moralism that could lead to the very condescension toward China that he found so appalling in his fellow Japanese. Attributing what he saw as Japan's backwardness to "slavish" borrowing, Takeuchi stressed only the moral aspects of Japan's war responsibility, and slighted the social-historical causes of the Second World War. Thus he came close to saying that one hundred million Japanese must confess their sins. While his analysis was transparently sincere, as a guide to the recent past it was weak.[46]

Still other critics thought it was far too late for Takeuchi's ideas of solidarity with China. Half a generation younger, the noted poet and critic Yoshimoto Takaaki thought that henceforth Japan and the West, not Japan and China, would have to face the crises of "post-modern" civilization together. "Asia" had been a useful concept once, perhaps, but was so no longer; and Yoshimoto suspected that Japan may have lived through its prewar-style emperor-centered nationalism and should henceforth have to share in the whole human predicament as he defined it, not just the Asian or Chinese portion of it. Marx had underestimated the staying power of the West, and what Yoshimoto feared was not Japan's estrangement from China, but the kind of emotionalism that he found in Takeuchi's concept of Asia, with its dangerously parochial overtones. What Japan needed now was not more exclusivist ethnic nationalism based upon some fictive "solidarity" with Asia but a "Marcusean revolution of the senses." For Yoshimoto history had a movement that seemed missing in Takeuchi's analyses.[47]

However, Takeuchi's mind was focused on Japan's national "failure." To exorcize that failure, rather than searching for innovative remedies in the realm of psychology or elsewhere, his brief was simple: Japan must experience a spiritual as well as social revolution separate in its essential spirit from the bourgeois West. He showed no signs of imagining that one day the Chinese themselves would turn toward modernizing goals. Nor did he ever say, if he understood it, that the Japanese, despite their obvious shortcomings, had used the strengths of their traditional qualities brilliantly to cope with the West and maintain their independence in the modern period; and that future independence could hardly come from withdrawal into some Chinese ideal but only by adapting Japanese strengths to the day-to-day needs of the universal marketplace of goods and ideas—in other words, by doing what most Japanese, leaders and people alike, were in fact doing after the war. For in spite of his apocalyptic vision, the samurai heritage, with its lineage of practical actors, not Lu Xun's abused villagers or Mao's peasant warriors or Gandhi's salt-marchers, was, for better or worse, what Japan had to work with in the postwar world.

As he became better known, Takeuchi's life grew more

settled. In 1949 he married and took a job as part-time lecturer in the literature department at Keiō University to supplement his income, but he never considered himself primarily an academic. He also accepted assignments to edit many collections of Chinese and Japanese writers. In 1953 he began an association that lasted for the rest of his life with the Institute of the Science of Thought (*Shisō no Kagaku Kenkyūkai*), one of the more important groupings of "progressive" intellectuals in Tokyo, which pioneered cooperative and other research projects on Japanese society after the war.[48] In the same year he became a professor of Chinese literature at Tokyo Municipal University, again as a means of supplementing income, and he was also active in civic organizations like the P.T.A. At least twice he was invited to visit China with cultural delegations, but declined, apparently to avoid identification with government policies.

As the 1950s passed, the legacy of the war for Takeuchi remained unexorcized. In article after article he dwelt bitterly on Japan's forced isolation from the mainland and continuing Japanese prejudice against the Chinese people. But as one critic wrote, insofar as the Japanese sought forgiveness from anyone, it was from America, not Asia.[49] Takeuchi's reason told him that Japanese modernism was a fact, and he even on occasion would call himself "half a modernist."[50] But in the same breath he also accused the United States of "unrighteousness" and agreed "seventy per cent" with his friend, Tsurumi Shunsuke, when the latter declared (during the Vietnam War) that "he who points a gun at America is my friend."[51] Eccentric as a "crane in a flock of chickens,"[52] Takeuchi pretended that Japan was "made possible" by China, and he proposed "Asia as a method" round which to build a new national and personal "independence" from the West. He was given to exhuming the reputations of people like Kita Ikki or Ōkawa Shūmei or the writers of the Romantic School (*Nihon Rōmanha*), finding a modicum of good in them where others found nothing to admire, and leading some of his more uncharitable critics to deplore his fondness for "fascists."[53] Occasionally he could be shaken by doubt: perhaps Japan was after all a legitimately "modern" society; if so, what was valid for China could never work there.[54] His thinking had a strongly either/or quality. He seems never to have considered that modern Japanese culture might be a composite of indigenous, Western, and Chinese elements in constantly changing equilibrium; and one critic found it "tragic" that he spent his whole career digging in his "Oriental heritage" while never appreciating that no amount of absorption in Chinese revolutionary fervor could ever raise such concepts to "world level."[55]

Takeuchi's last serious effort to sort out the problem of modernization and war guilt came in 1959 in an essay called "Overcoming the Modern" ("Kindai no Chōkoku").[56] In this piece he took as his text a wartime symposium attended by representatives of three well-known groupings of intellectuals: the Romantic School (*Nihon Rōmanha*) of writers and critics, the "Kyoto school" of philosophers and historians at Kyoto University, and writers associated with the literary magazine, *Bungakukai*.[57]

This symposium, famous in Japan, provides an interesting look into the impulse to reject the West, with all its painful as well as pleasurable consequences. As a wartime slogan to rally support for Japan's goals, "overcoming the modern" was a total failure, because no agreement could possibly ever be reached among Japanese intellectuals on the meaning of "modern." Some, like Kamei Katsuichirō, fulminated against all Western cultural influences, from the speed of automobiles to the supposed corruption of the Japanese language. Others, like Hayashi Fusao, mysteriously attributed the decline of modern Japanese literature to its increasing distance from the imperial throne. The professor of music, Moroi Saburō, thought modern musical composition had been cut off from "organic life"; Japanese music, like other aspects of the culture, had served too protracted an apprenticeship to the West; and, after all, had not European music since Beethoven been downhill all the way? Yet Moroi noted with chagrin that the West (or the "modern"—the terms were used interchangeably) could hardly be "overcome" by denying it. Overcoming the modern might mean overcoming Europe, but, asked the philosopher

Shimomura Toratarō, was not Europe "inside the Japanese" already, in mind and to a degree in spirit as well? Did not Japan share the "modern malady" with the West? And while it might be comforting to talk of some "Oriental extinction of the self," some need for "denial" and "silence," some compulsion to call Asia the "shadow" of the West, there was little point in trying to deny what was already partially absorbed, however poisonous modern life might appear to the "Japanese spirit."[58]

Takeuchi's analysis of this symposium constituted a kind of dance in the ruins of wartime "thought." He admitted that as an ideology for fighting a war against the West, the phrase "overcoming the modern" was without substance and its meaning forever obscure.[59] With one part of his mind he viewed such an archaic slogan with distaste. Yet at the same time he sympathized with the plight of the symposium participants, most of whom were hardly the fire-breathing ultranationalists they had been made out to be after the war. At bottom, he was convinced that the Asian part of the human race never could or should be wholly subsumed under the rubric "modern." A half-anachronistic figure himself, frustrated by his country's postwar foreign policies and ambivalent toward the whole temper of modern times as he saw them, Takeuchi had constructed a dilemma for Japan between East and West and dwelt there personally for more than twenty years. Defeat and Occupation, both imposed from without, had brought him no real solution to his nostalgia for the Chinese revolution and the profound malaise which he felt toward a Japan he took to be spiritually adrift in Asia. To him it was baleful that the majority of his people, who pushed for all-out modernization, science and progress, and the minority of nay-sayers with their "dark vision" of Asia, had never since 1945 had a chance to resolve their debate by themselves. He deplored official attitudes of superiority toward Asia: the Foreign Ministry continued to look down on China and ran servilely after the Western world. It was just such a mind-set that had led to disaster before, and might again. And he quoted Odagiri Hideo's warning: "We haven't worked to settle the past with our own hands, so the past is beginning to take its revenge on us."[60]

Finally, in this article he sought somehow to justify the war and rationalize it in a way that would retrieve some emotional satisfaction, even as his reason told him such rationalization was impossible. In the process, he resurrected Kamei Katsu-ichiro's interpretation of the war as having two aspects:

> Kamei rejected the notion that the war was one and indivisible and accepted responsibility only for the Asian portion of it. On this point alone I want to support his ideas. The Greater East Asia War was a war of colonial invasion and also a war against imperialism. These two aspects, in actuality one, should be separated in theory. Japan did not plan to invade America and England. Colonies were taken from Holland, but there was no attempt to take Holland. Imperialism cannot defeat imperialism, but neither can imperialism pass judgment on imperialism. To judge imperialism there has to be a general standard of values that all can accept, such as the Western belief in freedom, righteousness and humanism at the Tokyo trials. But . . . to Kamei such a standard of values was outside the Japanese tradition and merely smacked of the West.[61]

But if Kamei—and Takeuchi—refused to accept Western standards for judging Japan's acts, Takeuchi was also forced to recognize that neither was any other standard available during the war that might have been acceptable to other Asians to explain his country's war on the West. Only at the Tokyo trials did a possible standard emerge in the dissent of the Indian Justice Pal, who found the Japanese defendants innocent on all counts of charges based upon Western definitions of aggressive war. But Pal's judgment came long after the fact; the attacks on the West and on China had been pursued as inseparable parts of the same war. Takeuchi in the end recognized this: "In the Pacific war both aspects . . . were inseparably stuck together."[62] His effort to rationalize the war ended without success; yet, in Yoshimoto Takaaki's words, European logic was "bleak" to Takeuchi,[63] and one is left with the strong feeling that for him the "modern" was never either "over-

come" or accepted, and that in his heart he brooded to the
end and was perplexed over Japanese modernity and its losses,
and held emotionally to the conviction that "Asia is Europe's
food."[64] In any event, "Overcoming the Modern" was his last
attempt to dispose of war on paper. The next installment of
his story was to be characterized by greater political activism.

IV

In 1960, Takeuchi was fifty years old, a mature "progressive
man of culture" with many books behind him and a substantial
reputation in Tokyo intellectual circles. Not long after this he
estimated his steady readership at three hundred to five hundred people; but this referred only to the core membership of
the study groups with which he was affiliated, and was probably much too modest.

For many years his dissatisfaction with his own government
had been profound. He constantly inveighed in a variety of
journals against Japan's isolation from Communist China, and
blamed Japan's governors, the commercial, political and bureaucratic elite responsible for national policy-making. America to him was not wholly bad; democracy had had some
beneficial effects in Japan, but he knew very little about the
liberal West and had little curiosity about it. (He never visited
western Europe or America.) Until Japan understood the Chinese revolution, its national future would remain dark: for
"those who look down on others inevitably debase themselves
before others."[65]

He spoke these words in a public lecture on December 1,
1959. The Japanese government had been voluntarily negoti-
ating a new Security Treaty with the United States for many
months, and was on the point of signing a new treaty document
in Washington. In Tokyo, meanwhile, the movement against
the treaty led by students, labor unions and leftwing parties,
was well advanced, and for some time Takeuchi had been an
active member of opposition organizations. In 1958 he wrote
and spoke at a "people's congress" against the proposed

revision of the Police Duties Law, a measure which would have expanded police powers of arrest and search, but which was withdrawn after public protest. In March 1959 he joined other "men of culture" in a statement against the Security Treaty (*Ampo*) and in October of that year participated in the "Association for Criticism of the Treaty" (*"Ampo Hihan no Kai"*) and set up a "Treaty Problems Study Society" (*"Ampo Mondai Kenkyūkai"*) at Tokyo Municipal University. He was, in the phrase of one commentator, "entering practical activity."[66]

For Takeuchi the new Security Treaty had to be opposed because it would delay indefinitely the restoration of peace and friendly relations with mainland China. He approved but was less interested in other more general motives for blocking the treaty based on the desirability of Japanese neutralism. He could not be expected to foresee that in years to come the Beijing government would be glad for the Security Treaty as a hedge against Soviet-induced destabilization in Asia; in 1960, for the Japanese government and people voluntarily to accept a new treaty of alignment with the United States seemed to him a positive evil.[67]

The treaty was signed in Washington in January 1960 and soon afterward went into debate in the Japanese Diet. By April, Takeuchi was making grim pronouncements: "We must show our determination in action. If the government does not change its policies, we must overthrow the government." As often happens in these circumstances in Japan, military language crept into his writing: "If the present operation [*sakusen*] succeeds, we may prevent ratification."[68] As the Diet session ran out in May, he grew more agitated, excoriating government violence (but not student violence) and repeating rumors that the Self-Defense Forces had received orders to mobilize and that American forces might even be used.

On the afternoon of May 18, when the regular Diet session appeared on the verge of expiring without ratification of the treaty by the Lower House, Takeuchi joined a delegation of eleven intellectuals and "men of culture" who called upon Prime Minister Kishi personally and made representations against the treaty. The meeting was tense, but Kishi reassured them that their government would act in a responsible way.[69] Takeuchi's consternation may therefore be imagined when, at around midnight of May 19, he heard on his bedroom radio the news that the Liberal-Democratic Party had called out the police to remove Socialist members who were conducting a sit-down maneuver on the House floor, then railroaded through an extension of the Diet and passed the treaty with little regard for parliamentary niceties.[70] His immediate reaction was typically emotional: "Democracy is over, fascism is here."[71] A good many Tokyoites that night agreed with him. Thoughts of emigrating or even renouncing his citizenship went through his mind—later he would be embarrassed to think that he had ever had such ideas. Two days later he handed in his resignation from his teaching position.

Why did he not stay on and try to protect the Constitution from within the system? His action was entirely consistent with his earlier fondness for dramatic gestures; he wished to call public attention to dictatorial tactics of the government, and must have known he would gain more attention by resigning than by staying at his job. In the perfervid atmosphere of May/June 1960, resigning was the deed of a self-conscious intellectual, calling a corrupt regime to account. Here was his chance to put his dreams of a "protest society" inspired by Lu Xun into practice, a chance to register his name against the regime in a way that he had not done during the war. Above all, resigning was a personal, individual act; as he himself emphasized, "We should not think of the power of organizations by professional or occupational class, but must reduce everything to the character and nature of the individuals who make them up."[72]

With his resignation Takeuchi turned to full-time pamphleteering in the *Ampo* crisis. After May 19 the treaty itself became a secondary issue to him; what mattered was the government's "coup d'état" of that night, and the "dictatorship" he feared had arrived. (He did not appear to realize that his freedom to write and agitate as he did said something about the sturdiness of Japan's democratic political institutions.) After mid-May he

called in article after article for the citizens to take back
sovereignty into their own hands, where the Constitution had
placed it, and he argued passionately for participatory democracy: "Only those politicians who cooperate with the 'people's
movement' are the true representatives of the people, regard-
less of party."[73] The intellectuals' role in the struggle was to
help the people conquer their "slave mentality" and recover
what was theirs. As the crisis intensified in early June he shied
away from the use of violence, and worried that the police
might not be able to contain the demonstrations.[74]

Though his writings contained the usual leftwing phraseol-
ogy about "monopoly capitalism" and "dictatorship," the
main impulse of his protest was concern for the nation. In his
outrage against his own leaders, China for once dropped out
of his vocabulary. He turned rather to the Japanese past for
emotional support and resonance: "I am a postwar public
official [i.e., professor] but in my consciousness remain the
traces of Meiji and Taishō. Beyond that is a pattern of individualistic [koseiteki] thought and action that comes from my
temperament and education."[75] At moments in the struggle he
evoked imagery of popular solidarity that seemed as much a
cry for a lost Japanese community (kyōdōtai) as for revolution,
Chinese-style. At one moment he wanted to build a new Diet
with his own hands that would be based on the postwar
Constitution[76] but at another he had to admit that the new
Constitution seemed distant (yosoyososhii) from him: "It
stresses universal human rights, and that is wonderful, but I
have the feeling that it is too dazzling [mabushii] and I am
embarrassed to call it my own. . . . Are we such fine people?"[77]
And he plays with the suggestion that for his generation, at
least, it might have been more comfortable to try to express
their individuality under the bad old system, albeit that expression had to take distorted forms: "I do not say that the old
Constitution was good, but the new one is cold."[78]

By early June 1960, Takeuchi no longer was writing about
overthrowing the Kishi "dictatorship" but about making the
Constitution more "warm" to the people: "Even if Kishi were

overthrown, a second or third Kishi would be the only result."[79] His temper rose again on June 10 when James Hagerty, President Eisenhower's press secretary and advance man for Eisenhower's planned visit to Japan, arrived at Haneda airport only to be marooned by a mob that surrounded his car. Takeuchi quickly accepted the leftists' unsubstantiated claim (which Hagerty later denied) that Hagerty's car had been driven at full speed into the crowd of demonstrating students.[80] But what really irked him was Hagerty's reported remark that students who were singing the "Internationale" at Haneda that day thereby showed that they had no loyalty to Japan:

> Does Mr. Hagerty think it is the part of a foreigner to instruct a Japanese in his loyalty toward Japan? As a Japanese, I cannot tolerate the spiritual tampering in such a statement. It shows the greatest contempt for the Japanese people.[81]

And he claimed that the students had been singing merely to try to calm other demonstrators.

After the automatic Diet ratification of the treaty in late June, the period of post mortems began. Looking back in a series of articles, he felt that a great deal had been achieved by the anti-treaty movement. He realized that his resignation had been irrational; no revolution had occurred; but large numbers of Tokyo people had "picked up democracy" and made it their own. This was the first Japanese protest movement worthy of the name in modern times. Popular pressure for independence from America had proven in the event to be less intense than hatred of reactionary leaders at home; and there was no use in trying to see in the treaty movement a united Japanese-Chinese struggle against imperialism: Japanese nationalism was more complicated than that.[82] Nevertheless, the movement had produced a singular sense of solidarity among citizens from all walks of life and political persuasions;[83] and he professed to believe that the movement would ultimately bring Japanese closer to other Asians: "By their sincere struggle on May 19, a self-confidence was born in the Japanese people that they could carve out their destiny with their own power. This self-confidence pervades Asian and African nationalism, and is a prime mover of tomorrow's world."[84]

Later he grew even more mellow: the "movement" had brought down the Kishi cabinet, but Japan was far from ready to throw over parliamentary government:

> Democracy with all its phony aspects is a part of the legacy of modern Japanese history. One may talk about how democracy was given to us after the war, but in the individual's visceral feelings there is a considerable sense of his own rights. . . . Those in whatever opposition movements should ask themselves what they can achieve unless they base their position on this fact. . . .[85]

He gave two cheers for democracy, confessing that he had little confidence in it, and seldom used the word in his writings; on the other hand, it was "neither correct nor fruitful" to say that Japan's parliamentary government was "nothing more than a form of bourgeois dictatorship."[86]

On June 30, 1960 Takeuchi was retired at his own request and moved quietly into the post-*Ampo* era. By early 1961 his routine was back to normal. He became a member of the preparatory committee for an Asian-African writers conference in Tokyo, served on the magazine *Shisō no Kagaku*'s board of directors, and remained active in the P.T.A. at Kichijōji Primary School. His activities from 1960 until his death in 1977 formed a kind of coda to his earlier career. He wrote more essays, but nothing of major importance. He remained active as a translator, undertaking to do the complete works of Lu Xun, a project that remained uncompleted at his death. In 1964 he launched another magazine, called simply *China (Chūgoku)*, to serve as an outlet for his translations and miscellaneous writings.

He still took intellectual positions and made gestures. When *Chūō Kōron* in December 1961 balked at its usual responsibility for printing an issue of *Shisō no Kagaku* that dealt with the imperial institution, he supported the latter magazine's deci-

sion to go independent and broke off all relations with *Chūō
Kōron*. When a little later a proposal by American foundations
to grant major subsidies for modern Chinese studies in Japan
to be administered through the *Tōyō Bunko* met with a storm
of disapproval in some intellectual circles, Takeuchi took a
relatively temperate position, noting that earlier support for
Japanese natural and social science from the United States had
not provoked such an uproar, but implying that scholarly
subsidies needed to be considered as part of the deeper issue
of Japan's alignment with America.[87] When the Chinese ex-
ploded a nuclear device in 1964 he joined a group of intellectuals to issue a criticism of the event, but was careful to point
out that all nations must refrain from such behavior if peace
was to be insured. In 1972, aged 62, he still believed that Japan
and China somehow had a common destiny vis-à-vis the West,
albeit that destiny had been frustrated by the course of postwar
history.[88] Almost up to the moment of Japan's rapprochement
with China in 1972 he still regarded it as impossible.

With his health beginning to fail after 1960, he still hoped for
"maturity" (*seijuku*), felt that he lacked "system," and had
been merely a "half-way critic, half-way scholar, half-way
educator." He lectured in the provinces and had his feelings
hurt when nobody had read his books in Kesennuma, a coastal
town north of Tokyo. In the mid-60s he went on a brief tour of
eastern Europe via central Asia with his old friend and China
associate, Takeda Taijun. Most of all, in his later years he
developed a great love of skiing, going with family and friends
to the slopes in the Tōhoku, dressed fashionably in an expen-
sive Austrian jacket and French skis. Kept at home with an
ankle broken while skiing, he passed the time decorating a
Christmas tree for his younger daughter.

During the Vietnam War he gave money in support of
Beheiren (the League for Peace in Vietnam), which assisted in
the desertion of American soldiers; and he saw the United
States losing the war from the first, just as the Japanese,
lacking a base of support in the Chinese countryside, had
"inevitably" lost in the 1940s.[89] But he did not take active part
in this organization, and with age he lost interest in "move-

ments." He made light of the excesses of the Cultural Revolution, seeing it unexceptionably as an "inevitable" consequence of the struggle between Mao's desire to fight growing bureaucratism and remake Chinese society as a part of the "permanent revolution," and the instinct of other Chinese leaders to preserve the goals of conventional nationalism.[90] When Prime Minister Tanaka went to China in 1972 to reach "normalization" with Premier Zhou Enlai, Takeuchi welcomed the event but warned that the language of the joint communique was full of ambiguities and could lead to differences of interpretation. To his death in 1977 he never ceased to repeat that the Japanese had undervalued Chinese nationalism; until this attitude changed, Asia's future would be obscure.[91]

V

Set in a temporal frame, Takeuchi Yoshimi in Japanese terms belongs unambiguously to the prewar generation (*senzenha*). The war was the definitive event of his life, but his education was completed and his ideas formed before it, during the ascendancy of Japanese militarism and ultranationalism; he shared in the allegiances and doubts of a generation working under that shadow, and he reacted to release from it in complex ways. Perceived by his peers after the war as a serious-minded nationalist, he brought into focus a widely held feeling that the borrowing of half-digested ideas from the West in the pursuit of a modern society had derogated from Japanese pride and self-respect. His specific "Chinese" solution was unacceptable to most, yet on the issue of modernization he filed a minority report that was greatly admired. One colleague thought he had "reinforced his selfhood."[92] Another bought multiple copies of his essays and sent them to his friends.[93] Another called him a "fixed point" in an era of fickle values.[94] Still another reported that he had heard that former Prime Minister Kishi had expressed a desire to hear Takeuchi lecture on communist China, and thought this was not surprising![95]

Being identified with China carried its own special burden. Loving that country and its people himself, he was heir to an ambiguous legacy of Japanese admiration and contempt, of support for the goals of the Chinese revolution and manipulation of that revolution for Japanese ends. At the very least, lifelong identification with the study of modern Chinese literature and politics gave a special "Asian" flavor to his nationalism and set him apart from the mainstream of seekers after Western "enlightenment."

In other respects Takeuchi was typical of contemporary Japanese intellectuals. Most of his career was spent in private pursuits, first as a scholarship student in China in the 1930s, and later, in the 1950s, as a lecturer in a public university. Like many other intellectuals he was a bourgeois individualist who clung stubbornly to a view of himself as a loner, yet he also enjoyed throughout his career the company and support of a very Japanese kind of coterie of followers, in which he clearly played the role of father-surrogate. He wrote a great deal about culture, but he had little to say about specific institutions; his view of some institutions, such as education, was distinctly conservative. He said less than many about the emperor; the mechanics of politics hardly interested him, except perhaps for a few weeks in 1960. His revolution was a psychic event, a reconstruction of the inner being, the mental life. Like many other intellectuals he assumed a self-conscious responsibility for giving a lead to the people and changing their lives from within; he saw himself in some degree as a sage, but the specifics of his sagely prescriptions for social and political change were not laid out in much detail.

Takeuchi's writings bear witness to the power of China as an ideal society in the imagination of some Japanese after 1945, as well as the latent force of anti-modern impulses in those who grew to maturity before the war. His espousal of a somehow moral East versus a less than moral West exposed him to criticism as rather old-fashioned. Younger intellectuals naturally would have a different view of Japan's war in Asia. For example, one critic, who was thirteen in 1945, wrote that he had never thought of Japan as having specially invaded

China, everybody in Asia had been oppressed in one way or another by the Japanese. When World War II was mentioned, most younger Japanese thought of the Pacific islands, not China. The same writer thought that Takeuchi's dialectical view of history as East-West struggle was passé and faulted him for not being sufficiently interested in power: he should have written about "little bureaucrats" like General Tōjō, not just about intellectuals like Okakura Tenshin or Lu Xun.[96]

But Takeuchi's encounter with Chinese life had come during Chinese communism's heroic phase: Lu Xun, Sun Yat-sen, the young Mao Zedong were his heroes; their writings and those of Westerners like Snow, Lattimore, Belden and other observers of the Yanan period were his adored texts.[97] Where other Japanese intellectuals might see China as infinitely backward and Mao as a parochial thinker whose exaltation of his peasant base resembled nothing so much as Japanese agrarian primitivism in the 1930s,[98] Takeuchi thought he saw a genuinely new society taking form, rooted in the individual's self-respect in the working group, a *kyōdōtai* or commonalty based on the commune rather than the traditional Chinese family.[99]

Looking at Japan through this idealized Chinese lens, Takeuchi exaggerated the continuity of Japanese political society from before the war. In the sharpening confrontations of the 1950s leading up to the Security Treaty crisis, he attacked his country's leaders on moral and psychological as well as political grounds. In his dislikes, too, he was characteristic. No one outdid him in his disgust for the older, discredited nationalism and such perceived symbols of it as Prime Minister Kishi. But beyond personal targets, it was the "slavish" imitativeness, the derivativeness of Japanese society that drew his sharpest scorn, even as other, Western observers of the same scene were finding resourcefulness, vigor and pride in some of the same cast of characters. Modernization had robbed Japanese culture of Mao's "unrobbable base," its pride in protest and self-assertion. Other intellectual physicians might coolly dissect institutions, but Takeuchi was no social scientist; and when he asserted that independence and pride of nationality could only be fulfilled by protest, he touched deep romantic emotions in many hearts. For it should not be forgotten that intellectual discourse during Takeuchi's era was dominated by fear: fear of the ugly past's returning, of involvement in the Cold War, of too much "modernization" or too little. Behind the fear lay considerable national weakness, but the fear was always greater than the weakness.

His most productive years fell between 1945 and 1960, when memories of repression and defeat were at their most bitter and dependence on the goodwill and help of the former enemy at its most galling. He gave expression in lucid style and with honesty to what a good many perceived to be the unresolved nature of the Japanese cultural situation: one famous intellectual credited him with having been the very first to insist on the importance of ethnic ideas after the war.[100] His basic views changed little over the years, in spite of great changes in the Asian political terrain. He wrote little about the Sino-Soviet split and its implications for Sino-Japanese relations, and he seemed blind to shifts of opinion within Japan, especially the rise of self-confidence along with growing prosperity. In fact, his whole mind-set was inappropriate to the movement of his times. His yearning for the "folk" was less than ever relevant to Japan's "post-modern" problems.[101] Even such an intellectual as Yoshimoto Takaaki, whose nativistic speculations about mining the emotional riches of the "people" were analogous in a way to Takeuchi's "China" as the engine of a self-respecting nationalism, was far more aware than Takeuchi was of the effects of modernization on the postwar Japanese personality.[102]

He had to a remarkable degree what is called *shin,* "heart," a quality of strength and centeredness that some might associate with an authoritarian personality.[103] His friends all commented on his firm, almost severe demeanor, his habit of long silences, as well as his talent for friendship.[104] To them, he was a "man for all seasons," one who, to borrow St. Paul's words, aimed at "rightly dividing the word of truth."

Japan has not acted from Takeuchi's premises. *Shūsai,* the ability necessary to succeed in job and world, still is most highly prized in Japan's meritocratic society. Takeuchi knew little of how nations behave. He refused to see that relations with China would one day resume, and sooner rather than later, without the kind of abject apologies for past wrongs that no Japanese Prime Minister was prepared to give. His sense of Japan as a failed society and his guilt for the war in China were to be overwhelmed even before he died in the vast roar of economic productivity and the accompanying slower but substantial social change.

Yet his vision of a transfigured society based upon a Chinese psychic paradigm, a society that, in Lu Xun's phrase, would "borrow a fire to cook its own meat," rather than a society evolving imitatively and "slavishly" along Western lines, gave him a special claim to notice in the intellectual history of mid-20th-century Japan. Even by those who disagreed with him he was perceived to have been one of the most distinguished intellectuals after the war, a senior officer if not a commanding general in the intellectual wars of the 1950s and 1960s. He would have been the first to admit that he had not thought through the details of his alternative model of national behavior in any logical way, but of the necessity for an alternative he had no doubt. Until the Japanese people came fully to terms with their past in China, until they finally exorcized the Second World War, they would never learn what he had learned from that country: namely, that colonizers can never understand the colonized; that pride and independence come only from protest, from a "welling up inside the culture,"[105] not from the "cool" analysis of foreign institutions; and that only through protest, which with the exception of May–June 1960 the Japanese have not yet chosen to experience, would they achieve a full sense of their identity in the world of the future.

1981

CHAPTER THREE

Intellectuals and "The People":
On Yoshimoto Takaaki

This essay examines the career and selected writings of Yoshimoto Takaaki, a contemporary critic and thinker whose reputation has been made largely outside the Japanese intellectual "establishment." While no simple scheme of classification can do justice to the diversity of Japanese intellectual types, it is clear that since 1945 most influential intellectuals who have written about their culture and society have been preoccupied in one way or another with Western knowledge or Western institutions and their adaptation to Japanse circumstances. A much smaller number of writers and thinkers have focused their study on modern China and found in the Chinese revolution their inspiration and, to some degree, their ideals of political and social behavior. The subject of the present essay, however, fits into neither of these categories. While he has received his quota of Western influences, Yoshimoto has engaged in a kind of intellectual "quest for autonomy," seeking his own and his nation's identity not through an exploration of Western or Chinese ideas so much as through writing about the sentiments, expressive language and emotional life of "the people."[1] He is not a cultural chauvinist caught up in the celebration of Japanese uniqueness; on the contrary, from the outset of his career he has been appalled by the damage done both in his own life and the lives of others of his generation by the unscrupulous manipulation of symbols from the Japanese past.

Starting from the fact of total national defeat in 1945, like many other intellectuals Yoshimoto was concerned with what went wrong, what "distortions" and "contradictions" had afflicted Japanese history, especially since the late 19th century, and how a new characterization of the culture might be achieved. With others he shared a common tendency toward personal and national narcissism. He saw Japanese culture to be a mixture of native and foreign elements, but unlike many others he did not find these synthetic qualities a source of future strength.[2] He rejected the views of those writers who espoused a greater and greater cosmopolitanism in an ever-modernizing Japan. Instead, in essay after essay since the late 1950s, he turned inward to imagery surrounding "the people" in his efforts to define a Japanese national identity.

In the late 1950s and 1960s Yoshimoto's critical essays, poems and volumes of his conversations with other intellectuals were published in rapid succession in Tokyo (the *Zenshū* by Keisō Shobō, subsequent volumes by Chikuma Shobō and various other firms—no English translations of his prose are known to exist). In this period, too, he came to the notice of such prominent intellectual figures as Maruyama Masao, Takeuchi Yoshimi and Tsurumi Shunsuke, and his reputation as a polemicist was made among younger professors and university students, who were stirred by his call for intellectual independence and self-reliance *(jiritsu),* especially during and after the Security Treaty crisis of 1960. Many were also moved by his use of the term, "the people," less as a political counter than as a metaphor for lost emotional closeness and solidarity. Much of his appeal lay in his fondness for such emotive language; but beyond that, his attitude toward "the people" was never one of explicit or implicit disapproval. Like others he deplored their heritage of authoritarianism in family and state, but he never saw them as responsible for Japan's defeat because of their weak grasp of the meaning of free institutions of the Western type; nor did he view them as inherently incapable of protest and liberation in the Chinese communist manner and thus as having "failed." Instead, he romanticized "the people" for their ability to suffer, endure, and survive the corruption and misgovernment of the political and intellectual elite in Tokyo.

In spirit Yoshimoto's long inquiry into his cultural roots was not so much moving toward a vision of Japan as one nation in a world of nations as it was groping inwardly for some restatement of a particular and separate identity. He clung to the notion of Japanese separateness, claiming that foreigners lacked the requisite degree of "despair" in their efforts to understand the country.[3] His writing about "the people" was often obscure; their role in the cosmos of his ideas about culture was never very precisely defined. Just as unclear was his perception of himself vis-à-vis them: he needed to feel some emotional closeness to them, but like most other intellectuals he also needed to keep them at arm's length, and the possibilities of condescension in his attitude toward them were consequently very great.

His ideas about "the people," which he said lay at the core of his thought, had no sustained political consequence. He built no system, proposed no special theory, but persistently exalted the notion of emotional solidarity between intellectuals and "ordinary" Japanese. Like the American poet Carl Sandburg, he proclaimed "the people, Yes!" He was a symptom of the pluralistic intellectual search for cultural identity that accompanied economic recovery and political confrontation in the postwar period, and especially in the decade 1955–65. In his later writings he seemingly abandoned "the people" in favor of abstruse speculations on the psychology of perception and excursions into esthetics. Yet he sounded a note that appealed, especially to the young: Miura Masashi, the youthful editor of the intellectual journal *Gendai Shisō,* which printed a number of essays by and about Yoshimoto, insisted that Yoshimoto's charisma remained great among university students. In his stress on independence and a return to the emotional life of "the people," as well as in his diatribes against such establishment intellectuals as Maruyama Masao, he provoked widespread attention among many who felt the continuing strain of Japan's peculiar cultural situation.

I

Yoshimoto Takaaki (Ryūmei) was born in Tokyo in 1924, the third son of a shipwright who managed a small boatyard. Shortly before his birth the family had migrated from their home in southern Kyūshū, settling down on the waterfront at the mouth of the Sumida River in Chūō Ward. Yoshimoto's earliest memories were of this bayside landscape: the taste of silverberries *(gumi)* picked on trips with his father to the harbor's artificial islands, the gleaming handlamps and pick-axes of dock construction workers, the gear of a street repair gangs. In the rebuilding city a year after the great earthquake the Yoshimoto family were poor outsiders and regarded as such; at the same time they were somewhat envied by earlier arrivals in the city for their unspoiled down-country accents.[4] The young Yoshimoto felt apart from the first: "I was taught to think of my distance as a condition of being, necessary evidence of my own self." Or, more bitterly, "Loneliness is nothing but good feelings toward others and the reverse reaction these feelings bring about."[5]

Graduating from primary school in 1937, the first year of full-scale war with China, Yoshimoto moved through middle school and industrial higher school, the latter in Yamagata Prefecture, where he went because he wanted independence from his family in Tokyo.[6] The Tōhoku climate and landscape affected him deeply. He loved the mountains and the snow, and there he began writing poetry, read translated Western novels, and admired the poets Miyazawa Kenji and Takamura Kōtarō and the novelists Yokomitsu Riichi and Dazai Osamu. In 1944, inspired by Miyazawa's dreams of an agrarian utopia to be achieved through improved agricultural methods, he returned to Tokyo and enrolled in the chemical engineering course at Tokyo Engineering University. In the spring of 1945 he was mobilized for war work and sent to a Nihon Carbide

Company factory in Toyama Prefecture; and there, on August 15, 1945, in the courtyard of the plant, he listened to the Emperor's radio broadcast announcing Japan's total capitulation. Soon thereafter, he returned to Tokyo, sold his books and began reading other works on Buddhism and the Japanese past; after a time he attended lectures again and graduated from the university in the fall of 1947.[7]

After a childhood of unquestioning acceptance of what he had been told about his country and its mission in the world, Yoshimoto was stunned by Japan's defeat. His wartime verses exalting the "fatherland's battle" had totally supported war against the Anglo-Saxon powers.[8] When he heard the news of the fall of Saipan, Iwojima and Okinawa in successive bitter battles, he was not disposed to accept defeat meekly but was fired by the same chauvinistic spirit as Takamura Kōtarō, who wrote, "Let all Japanese arise and send their blood to the Ryūkyūs!"[9] Given this defiant attitude, the effect on him of the Emperor's broadcast was bound to be devastating: he had been wholly committed, and his principal reaction to defeat was a sense of overwhelming personal betrayal, which permanently reinforced his conviction that the particular wartime experiences of his adolescent age-group had been unique, unshared and unsharable by all Japanese even a little older or younger than himself. To this was joined a natural, if rather naive, suspicion that nearly all others of whatever age must also have been taken in and had no genuine claim to have opposed emperor-centered nationalism. The fact of defeat thus became the starting-point in the history of his maturing consciousness; out of defeat came whatever liberating changes were to occur in Japanese life, whether from internal or external causes, and the subsequent failure of the Japanese to turn defeat into social revolution merely showed their inability, or so he felt, to be truly independent after the war as before it.[10] Defeat gave a special meaning to the phrase "war generation" *(senchūha),* a term invested with a mystique of subjective shock differentiating otherwise unexceptionable lives.

Thus armed with an original sense of his own and his family's separateness as well as the conviction that he was a victim, Yoshimoto was ejected into the confusion of the immediate postwar period. After leaving the university he worked for some months in a small factory manufacturing insulation materials, but quit because working conditions began to affect his health. He then found work in a chemical plant, but lost this job in a dispute over the formation of a labor union. Out of work and grieving over the death of an elder sister, to whom he wrote several poems, he turned back to the university for a livelihood and became a research assistant at *Kōgyō Daigaku* doing chemical research. All during this time he was still living with his parents. Before long he went to work for the Tōyō Ink Company, one of the largest such concerns in the country. Throughout this whole period he had been writing poetry, and in 1952 his first noteworthy book of poems, *Koyūji to no Taiwa,* was published.

He soon became involved again in union organization at the ink plant, which led to a loss of confidence in him by his employers, but he remained with Tōyō Ink for several years until, after having been shunted from section to section and finally put in a new "planning section" where he was the only employee, he resigned. He was 31, and appeared to believe that his chances of succeeding in the capitalist mainstream of Japanese society were over.[11] After quarreling with his father over quitting the ink company job, he found part-time work in an office issuing patents and licenses, where he was put to work translating documents from German. In 1956, after years of poverty, he married and appeared to be stabilizing his life to some degree, just as the Japanese economy as a whole was beginning its phenomenal expansion. Soon thereafter he became the father of a daughter, and in 1958 his *Collected Poems* was published. For many years thereafter he was to publish relatively little poetry.

Yoshimoto's early postwar writings revealed a self-absorbed young man given to speculation about his relation to the universe, fond of declamatory statements about God, Time and Mankind, but weak in engagement with specific men, times or situations—in short, a youthful idealist in whom there was little discernible movement out of the self. His life purposes were still vague: "My life was not for achieving any end, I was merely to add something"—what, he did not yet know.[12] There was no doubting that his early life on the Tokyo waterfront left him with diffuse romantic identifications with working-class people, which were to become more noticeable in his later writings and which were fed in part by his early encounter with the poetry of Miyazawa Kenji, the idealist poet whose life had to some extent empitomized service to the common people of the rural north.[13]

Yet in spite of his lower-middle-class origins, in many respects Yoshimoto resembled other young Japanese of his own age and educational level, and there is little evidence that any self-conscious feelings of class were significant in shaping his early ideas. More important than class was a personal tendency from childhood to cling combatively to positions taken[14] and a keen awareness of generational differences, especially the notion that the wartime experiences of his precise contemporaries conveyed a special license for disillusionment and the exposure of false positions in others. His rather romantic quest for self-location in the shifting ethical terrain of the early postwar period was typical of many university students of whatever generation, albeit perhaps more intense in Yoshimoto than in the average case. His ruminations on his existential plight went over familiar ground, and hardly reverberated with the slogans of class struggle:

> Any man must have work. How many times I have said this to strengthen myself. And now I still have none. . . . This is the cruelly harsh fact. . . . Marx, Bakunin, LaSalle, Oppenheimer, F. List, Arthur Rimbaud, Paul Valéry, André Gide . . .[15]

He seems to have drawn nourishment from writing down such lists of names, a litany of the foreigners who perhaps preoccupied him at that point. But along with Rodin and St. Augustine, he was also reading the *Ise Monogatari* and writing verse on themes that were hardly Western:

Pilgrim Song I

The sleeve written round with Sanskrit characters
Smells of rain. . . .

> A figure of unparalleled loneliness
> With your priest's staff knocking along
> Leaving this lonely street
> With the snow not yet melted
> Will you cross Funazaka Pass? . . .[16]

Other excerpts from his writings of the late 1940s may help to convey something of his mental outlook; they reveal a sensitive temperament and a mind given to stock attitudes of deprivation but little class feeling:

> Society is a collection of numberless, disorderly oppressions. . . . Order is another word for exploitation. . . . Freedom can only be found when it hits against something. . . . Thought derives only from experience. . . . Early spring is the season of unbearably heavy hell. . . .[17]

Or again:

> To find the way to individuality is hard. Youth can never be individualistic; which is why youth dies from illusion. . . . History shows that the lower classes must escape from all political, economic and moral control.[18]

After the Korean War began in June 1950 he made one of the relatively few references in his work to the world beyond Japan:

> The world is in the midst of despair. If the products of the human spirit have cast that spirit into despair, that is something for which Europe is responsible. Asia has made no essential contribution to it at this stage. Asia's despair is despair against the reality that prevents its own awakening.[19]

In the early 1950s Yoshimoto turned from poetry and began to write essays and critical articles. His most pressing questions at this time were ethical ones: what values should one live by, what is the Good, and where can it be found? Soon he read the New Testament, no doubt in part as a reaction against the suffocations of the nationalism he had been taught in wartime. A direct result of this encounter was the long "Draft Essay on the Book of Matthew" (1954), one of his first serious attempts to find answers to questions about the conduct of life.

In this piece he advanced the notion that Matthew had invented Jesus as the founding figure of a new sect to embody Jewish myths about the leader of an oppressed people. "[Jesus] is the hero of the story created by the 'Messiah outlook'; there is no evidence of his existence as a man in the history of human thought."[20] A creation of Matthew's imagination, Jesus' life was made to fit in with apocalyptic legends and to perform supernatural acts related to Old Testament prophecies. Already conceiving his own position as one of the oppressed and alienated, Yoshimoto interpreted the ethics of Jesus as a means of opposing the social order but was repelled by what he took to be the Christian flight from reality, from the ineluctable facts of history, into an ideal order of the feelings. He rejected out of hand the whole idea of Christian faith: "Is not all that derives from faith evil? Faith comes not from human thought, but it robs that thought of meaning."[21]

The theology of Matthew ultimately was abhorrent to the young Yoshimoto because it was "unnatural." He interpreted the development of the idea of sin as the product of the psychic condition of the early Christians, the result of their persecutions and betrayals, for which he had sympathy; but again and again he rejected the teachings of Matthew for their "unnaturalness":

> Nothing describes the contradiction between doctrine and actual human feelings as sharply as early Christianity. . . . When it says to love God, it knows very well that the actual feeling in that love is very thin. There is a connection between man and man, and that is all there is in actuality. For that reason, to give any actuality to loving God, it is necessary to be supported by feelings of harsh opposition against the whole of actuality.[22]

In the early postwar period strategies of protest such as the early Christians used may have seemed transiently relevant to some Japanese intellectuals in reaction against the frustrations of a failed ultranationalism. But Yoshimoto's interest in the Christians was more psychological than political; Christian consciousness was a coat to try on for matching existential ideas or states of mind more than it was a program of actual revolutionary possibilities.

"Matthew" appeared in 1954, a year full of perversity for Yoshimoto. Relations with his family were strained, he was on his way out of the ink company, and his interest in writing poetry was declining. From the first, his poems had been exceedingly private, spun out of himself, often in the form of ruminative monologues. At their best they communicated insights about man-in-nature, but they were often opaque in their self-absorption, and the youthful self he had to offer was, in the nature of things, not particularly compelling. Though he professed to be deeply moved by the wholeness of humanity in Miyazawa Kenji's work, his own poetry did not display anything comparable to Miyazawa's arresting idiom. He could occasionally communicate passionate feeling,[23] but for the most part his lyric efforts slid away from contact with the world of the concrete toward abstraction.

His biographer indicated that he moved in the direction of critical writing and concern for the ethic of rebellion shortly after his marriage in 1956. Probably there were economic reasons for this. At all events, he had read Marx earlier along with the Bible; both were in a sense obligatory influences; and with Christian transcendence rejected, the way seemed open to embrace some other system of belief within history.[24] Marx pointed the way to a secular utopia, a sanction for Yoshimoto's romantic compulsion to identify with the oppressed without the need to become involved in any uncongenial, unprovable religious faith. Marx was not Jesus "unnaturally" turning the other cheek to his revilers; his multitudes were more contemporary, more "relevant." Marx showed Yoshimoto the injustice of the historical universe and turned him toward the real world as the Bible did not.[25] Yet his biographer also called Yoshimoto a "Miyazawa Kenji who knew Marx,"[26] no doubt wishing to suggest that he was above all a poet and a man of humble origins who felt compassion for the common people.

Somewhat later, in 1964, Yoshimoto published a long article on the early philosophical writings and details of the biography of Karl Marx. He readily accepted Marx's insights into alienation, the exploitation of the working class, and the "illusions" of society, notably the state. These ideas moved him as they did many other Japanese because they fit his view of his own world, in which, during his young manhood, the masses of the Japanese people had been shown to be politically passive and subject to manipulation. Aware of his own extreme circumstances after the war, and of his alienation from the mainstream of his society, he easily embraced a romantic desire for revolution to bring the masses to full consciousness of their historical situation. Yet for him the revolution remained as much a poetic event as anything more politically real. He felt the dialectic of class struggle weakly; distant from the trenches of class warfare, he inveighed against his country's leaders for their sins but always retained a sharp sense of his own individuality. Yet reading Marx led him toward his real vocation, which was for polemics, for the infighting of the intellectual guerrillas of postwar Tokyo. He himself realized this in reflecting on his later career:

> I first became fairly well absorbed by Marx's writings in the 1945-48 period, and then again some ten years later, and I wrote on the subject of Marxism during each of these experiences. What does Marx mean to me now [1966]? The shock was great when I first encountered this unknown world just after the war. But for some years now the "rescue" of Marx has been a strong imperative for me. By this I mean trying to save him from the old-style prewar left. They die embracing a false image of Marx. . . . I am still surprised that I can find no flaw in Marx; I am surprised by the volume of his ideas. Yet I can now see fairly well what he did and did not do, and I feel there is something reserved to me in the realm of ideas, and that my understanding of Marx was and is different from that of others.[27]

After reading Marx's early writings and, by 1950, *Das Kapital,* Yoshimoto in the middle 1950s plunged eagerly into the literary and political controversies of the time. Certain attitudes already were evident in his writing:

> Those I most despise are scholars, fashionable artists and garrulous powerholders. . . . It is unbearable that most of those I respected died [in World War II] while those I despise are safe whether in peace or war. . . . I disbelieve all who claim they were anti-war before 1945.[28]

While other "social science" intellectuals like Shimizu Ikutarō were leading demonstrations against American bases at Uchinada or elsewhere or taking up the anti-nuclear movement, Yoshimoto soon made a name for himself by his attacks on leftwing writers who had recanted their communist beliefs before or during the war and who, reemerging after 1945 as self-proclaimed liberal democrats, claimed to have opposed ultranationalism all along. While sympathetic with the goals of the postwar left, he was apprehensive from the outset about its failure to change its mind fundamentally about the emperor and the state. This now somewhat dated issue of recantation and collaboration *(tenkō)* became the vehicle by which Yoshimoto was to establish his reputation with a larger public.

In a 1958 article he suggested that although some leftwing writers and others might initially have been forced into apostasy by government repression and censorship in the early 1930s, there was another, deeper motive in recantation of communist beliefs, namely, a visceral yearning not to remain isolated from the emotional mainstream of Japanese sentiment as the country slid toward war with the Anglo-Saxon powers. And after 1937 this desire not to be cut off from the feelings of the *kyōdōtai* became a stampede as jingoism swept over the country.[29]

His attack on the prewar left was not limited to the apostasy issue alone; he also criticized those communist writers who saw art as mere political propaganda and agitation. He accused Miyamoto Kenji and other old-time communist leaders of mouthing the "slogans of mechanical Marxism" in their insistence that "class art is a form of the class struggle."[30] Yet neither could he accept the notion that the key to artistic value lay in the work alone; he rejected art for art's sake as well as art for propaganda, and proposed a more relative scale of judgement:

> Some art can be judged on political and ideological grounds, and this may be necessary in order to clarify its artistic value. The key to artistic value is not in the work itself, but in the internal consciousness of actuality of the person who judges. Hence for a certain judge, artistic value and political value may run along the same axis. . . . Thus when Tolstoi in the end clung to God and retained the sensibility of the landlord class, this can be seen as a minus or a plus, both artistically and politically, depending on one's point of view.[31]

Yoshimoto's criticism of communist writers on both political and esthetic grounds may have contributed to exploding the myth that communists had been the only true protestors against the war.[32] Yet because he had had no experience of the prewar intellectual situation under military rule, he was criticized for failing to penetrate the complexities of apostasy and collaboration. His criticism, by naming names, drew counterattacks from various quarters. Those who recognized him as a natural enemy were quick to call him a ''fascist.'' Other more measured students of the *tenkō* issue suggested that his rigid intolerance of those whom he believed had lied about their liberal tendencies might simply have reflected the extent of his own unquestioning comformity during the war. The same sources thought that he failed to appreciate the existence of a history of skepticism and varying degrees of feigned loyalty toward the regime—''false *tenkō*'' as a phenomenon may have eluded his understanding.

At all events, as a lonely and uncompromising critic of all power systems, Yoshimoto was regarded by his critics as a dogmatist who could not abide the thought that others were as pure as himself; some compared him with communists who had been expelled from the party, and even to Miss Havisham in Dickens's *Great Expectations,* who had been jilted by her betrothed and spent the remainder of her life in her room.[33] From the fastness of his own rather simpleminded purity, his critics implied, he lashed out at the presumed ideological inconstancy of others older and perhaps cleverer than himself. In the face of such attacks, cried Yoshimoto, "How can the despair of the young be dissipated?"[34] His own despair and hatred of Japan's postwar leaders had something about it of the intensity of Matthew's feelings toward the persecuting Jews.

Yoshimoto's writings of the late 1950s were marked by their high-pitched tone and their irritation at the way, or so he believed, intellectuals of various persuasions shifted their positions in a kind of ideological vacuum without reference to the "actual tendencies of the thought of the people."[35] The stress on "actuality" and "people's thought" became increasingly noticeable from about this time. He did not describe in any detail what he believed those words to mean, or what he offered to fill the "vacuum" he deplored. His complaints were highly articulated, his remedies murky. Yet he was launched on the polemical career of the professional intellectual and his impatience with his peers was very clear, as were the outlines of a confidence in "ordinary" people and their ideas about their lives. These themes had been anticipated by his childhood interest in Miyazawa Kenji and by his interpretation of *tenkō* in cultural terms as a return to the emotions of the larger community. This was the ground base toward which his arguments were to return again and again in the years that followed. By not fully confronting the basic, enduring problems of Japanese society, particularly the archaic "emperor-system" and the authoritarian structure of the family, both of which he believed persisted into the postwar era, intellectuals until the present had merely aped imported ideas—Christianity, Stalinism, Taishō "liberalism"—none of which, he thought, could really speak to the Japanese people's hearts; or, conversely, intellectuals had recoiled from all such foreign ideas to proclaim the superiority of nativistic ideas, the implications of which for the country they had never fully explored.[36] The intellectual vanguard or elite thus had failed to integrate the emotions and the *weltanschauung* of "the people" into its own thought; instead, intellectuals drifted, empty and dysfunctional, between the ruling classes and "the people." In so doing they misjudged "the people's" resilience:

> The war destroyed the people's living and their spirit. But the society's material structure has expanded. The masses of the Japanese people may never easily grasp universal rationality [*sekai risei*], but through material growth the modernization of mass society is likely to recover quickly. The self-consciousness of literary intellectuals is far too highly valued, while the self-consciousness of the people and their war scars are not valued highly enough.[37]

More orthodox Marxist critics may have had such passages in mind when they called Yoshimoto a "late-stage modernist."[38] Yet he was far from espousing received modernization theory, and he regarded as naive those who professed to believe that the "contradictions" of society would be resolved merely by modernizing traditional social structure along Western lines.[39] He saw Japan to be in the grip of monopoly capitalism and thought that land reform had been a mere ploy of the American Occupation forces to keep the Japanese market safe for international capital.[40] He believed that the capitalists and the bureaucrats would keep the farmers and small businessmen in thrall as long as there was no revolution. Yet the revolution was a less realizable hope by the late 1950s: the atmosphere of boom and the new assurance of the Japanese in the economic sphere did not escape him; and while in the late 1940s revolution and independence had seemed indivisible, already before 1960 he had begun to think of the postwar period as an opportunity for the Japanese people to achieve a wholly new kind of "independence" (*jiritsu*), even if they could not turn defeat in World War II into a social revolution.

Yoshimoto was increasingly to address the content and meaning of that "independence." But that was for the future; in the meantime, with his flag hoisted on the polemical sea, he

drifted toward the Security Treaty crisis of May–June 1960.
Although fundamentally disillusioned by the collapse of the
leftwing party movement under totalitarianism before and during the war, his own analysis of the situation in January 1960
was not unlike that of the Japanese Communist Party:

> The Security Treaty problem is to be understood as an agreement
> between the inner logic of Japanese capitalism's expansion and
> the international bourgeoisie's exploitative battle for markets. It
> cannot be explained by linkage with the daily struggle of the
> labor movement, nor has it anything to do with whether "our
> country" is servile or independent, or with the question of peace
> or war.[41]

As the controversy over treaty revision grew, Yoshimoto became actively involved in the "struggle": he spoke to a Zengakuren meeting in December 1959 and again in January 1960.
His writings about "the people" and the ethic of rebellion had
attracted some following among radical university students.[42]
The treaty crisis proper saw him in the streets. For once action
replaced ratiocination. On June 4 he participated in a sit-in at
Shinagawa station; on the night of June 15 he was inside the
Diet fence with Zengakuren students, harangued them during
the early hours of June 16, was pursued by the police in the
mêlée that followed and arrested for trespassing on the Diet
premises. He was held for two days and released.[43]

In October 1960 Yoshimoto wrote the first of several postmortems of the whole episode. He saw the effort to block
treaty revision to have failed utterly. In Japan the basis for
revolution did not yet exist. He condemned the behavior of
both communists and "progressives." The communists had
revealed their true colors during the riots: rather than go to the
defense of the students against the police they had held back
to preserve themselves "in being" and to sabotage the student
radicals and stymie the revolution.[44] They were reactionaries
beneath contempt. But even more pitiable, because more
naive, were the "progressive" or "enlightenment" *(keimō)*
intellectuals, who had been diverted from the true goal of

preventing treaty revision into an attack on the Kishi government and who afterward tried to save something from the
debacle by claiming that "democracy" had been rescued by
their protests and by Kishi's resignation. By late 1960 Yoshimoto felt more alienated than ever from such intellectuals, and
particularly from academic intellectuals, whether communist
or "progressive." The former were nothing but bureaucrats,
who "had no inner world to sustain their isolation from emperor-centered fascism" and who after 1945 had tried to foist
themselves on the public as self-styled champions of democracy and "citizens' literature."[45] The latter were mere Westernizers who sought to impose strange, alien ideas on "the
people."

Yet, despite the evident failure of the movement to block
treaty revision, to Yoshimoto the struggle had been worth-
while. The nameless masses' fight in May–June 1960 was more
important than the theories or "action policies" of sectarian,
bureaucratic intellectuals.[46] Street demonstrations had not
brought revolution, but that did not invalidate them. Rather
they taught a lesson: that it was best to keep "the people" and
the ideologues apart and to put one's faith in the former. "The
people" were to be trusted before the intellectuals.[47]

After the treaty crisis Yoshimoto also criticized what he
took to be Maruyama Masao's view that the postwar Japanese
had grown too privatized, that their privatization had led to
apathy toward electoral politics, and that this apathy stood in
the way of the development of parliamentary democracy in
Japan.[48] Yoshimoto conceived of politics differently. To him,
privatization was the very basis of "the people's" postwar
protest: the treaty crisis was proof, when the privatized selves
of thousands of ordinary students and citizens took to the
streets to vent their feelings of estrangement and alienation.
This was participatory, or true, democracy. And he extolled
the courage of the students (he was much less enthusiastic
about labor's role in the crisis) and felt guilt about his own
depth of commitment to the struggle. While he would have
been ready to give his life during World War II, he had not

been willing to do so to block the Security Treaty, and this troubled him.[49]

II

Behind Yoshimoto's dissatisfaction with other intellectuals and his need to identify with "the people" lay not only his combative temperament but also an awareness of his modest origins and, more generally, frustration over the direction and definition of Japanese culture in the postwar period. How to transcend the limitations of imported ideology on the one hand and nativistic Japanese ideology on the other and reach a new ideological synthesis became his increasing preoccupation after the Security Treaty crisis. In a 1962 article on nationalism he sketched the development of native ideas in the School of National Learning from Kamo Mabuchi's simple immersion in nature, through Motoori Norinaga's abstraction of nature as transcending man, to Hirata Atsutane's linkage of nature with the lives of the people, and Satō Nobuhiro's expansion of nature into a world-conquering ideology of Japanism, in which nationalism became "bourgeois and exclusivist." This "nature nationalism" had been tricked out as a unifying ideology in more recent times and given political and cultural force in the "emperor-system." Yoshimoto deplored the uses to which he conceived the *kokugaku* school had been put, but at the same time he stressed the latent power of *kokugaku* ideas in post-1945 Japanese sensibility and warned against the inadequate nourishment of the popular mind by imported, half-digested ideologies. He saw Japan's problem of cultural synthesis as to some degree similar to that of all late-modernizing states. Indigenous thought about self and society could not be turned into a ready-made internationalism simply by fiat; and just as the "emperor-system" had been used in the early 20th century to "strengthen and fatten" modern capitalism, so in the future one could not be sure what form nativistic ideas might take in the effort to come to terms with the world beyond Japan's shores. Prewar intellectuals had had nothing but foreign-tainted ideologies (Christianity, communism, liberalism) with which to fight the dark power of the "emperor-system" and the organic state. The results were history. But by the same token, being pro-Soviet or pro-American after the war told nothing whatever about the ultimate strength of Japanese ideas for either constructive or destructive purposes.[50]

Maruyama Masao, he wrote, attributed the failure of modern Japanese nationalism to its refusal to join either the democratic West or revolutionary China, and so to move toward one world or the other, but in any case, toward the world. But to Yoshimoto, the greater problem was that nationalism since 1945 had merely entered a Taoist phase, deprived for the time being of its old shibboleths of emperor and nature symbolism, defeated but not destroyed.[51] In another 1962 article he criticized Maruyama more frontally, taking him to task for not caring more for "the people." His critique of Maruyama had several levels. To begin with, he saw Maruyama as a dry academic who lacked Hegel's "bloody vision of history." In his treatment of Tokugawa ideas, Maruyama had exchanged "spirit" for "thought"; he was too cool, too concerned with "cycles of history" rather than the "bloody visage of mankind."[52] These flaws Yoshimoto attributed to Maruyama's supposed overintellectualization of his wartime experiences: although conscripted as a common soldier toward the end of the war, Maruyama had had no real understanding of other soldiers' lives or of popular feelings about the war; and Yoshimoto contrasted Maruyama's attitudes toward his fellow-soldiers with the hero in Tayama's famous novel about the Russo-Japanese War, *Ippeisotsu,* to the former's obvious disadvantage.[53]

On another level, Yoshimoto charged Maruyama with exaggerating the importance of Ogyū Sorai in his famous analysis of the breakdown of neo-Confucian categories of thought in the Tokugawa period in *Nihon Seiji Shisōshi Kenkyū.** As Maruyama stressed the significance of external order and

---

*Translated by Mikiso Hane as *Studies in the Intellectual History of Tokugawa Japan,* Princeton University Press, 1974.

political institutions in Sorai's outlook, so Yoshimoto clung to
Itō Jinsai's emphasis on ethics and his more intuitive "creative
power" by which to reach a kind of personal saintliness.
Dismissing Sorai as a mere tool of the ruling class, Yoshimoto
thought Jinsai had a far truer insight into the artificialities of
the neo-Confucian orthodoxy and how to naturalize it to
Japanese conditions.[54] In taking this line, he not only revealed
his temperamental uncongeniality with Maruyama, he also
dealt rather carelessly with Maruyama's scholarly method,
and he showed little or no appreciation of his analytical
achievements. He implied that Maruyama achieved clarity by
cutting out of his analysis "all the living masses of the people
who live by what is vague, irrational and hard to deal with."[55]
He seems to have thought that Maruyama had chosen Ogyū
Sorai as the key figure in the disintegration of the neo-Confucian world view simply because Sorai's stress on politics, his
separation of the public and private spheres, fit in with and
supported Maruyama's commitment to the essentially foreign,
transplanted discipline of political science.[56] Likewise he
seemed unable or unwilling to conceive that Japanese consciousness might have evolved through a long process of
historical development out of what Maruyama called the "con-
tinuative" mode in medieval times toward the divided consciousness which, for better or worse, was the ineluctable
condition of the modern mind.[57] He could not tolerate the
notion that Japanese intellectual history might have had and
might still be having a growth similar to, or at least analogous
to, the Western experience, or that, in the broadest sense,
Japanese experience might be converging toward the experience of the rest of the human race.

Maruyama emerged hardly diminished from Yoshimoto's
criticism. Maruyama's analysis of the shift in the center of
gravity of Tokugawa thought from "nature" to "artifice" or
"invention" remained a valid achievement in its own terms,
however his treatment of Sorai might be criticized in detail.[58]
What Yoshimoto's attack on Maruyama revealed was his own
growing need for some new formulation of the direction Japanese consciousness was to take in future, some satisfactory

description of "Japaneseness" that would not be a fusion of anything Japanese and Western, or Asian, either, for that matter. What would being Japanese mean in a Japan that had recovered economically and gone beyond any Western models, but whose relations with the rest of the world were still hesitant and weakly felt? It was probably too much to expect that Maruyama, an analyst of historical consciousness using the tools of social science, would have answers that would satisfy a poet like Yoshimoto, for whom an intuitive feeling for the integrated life of "the people" was more important than any objective analysis of their role in history.

As the 1960s passed, Yoshimoto's uncritical confidence in "the people" underwent some change. Partly this was an effect of the long shadow cast by the failure of the movement against treaty revision. But there was also a larger sense of disappointment. In his heart he came to feel more and more that man was in decline. With the rise of the mass media, knowledge proliferated but could no longer be equated with Marx's "act of consciousness."[59] With the breakup of the idea of the nation, Japan had merely come to mirror the fragmentation and divisiveness characteristic of the world as a whole. Such a situation was wrong. It was intolerable. Nothing could ever be solved by the confrontation of socialist and capitalist camps, both of which Yoshimoto increasingly disliked. Stalinism might decline into political apathy and mass consumerism, but the world would still be divided into haves and have-nots, and the few would still rule the many. The two power blocs would snarl at each other, while the masses would have left only apathy.[60]

This rather petulant sense of decline permeated his long article of June 1964, "Nihon no Nashionarizumu," in which he idealized the early Meiji period as a time of bourgeois revolution, when feelings of patriotism had been mobilized behind such catch-phrases as *risshin shusse* (success in life) and the hard-work-and-frugality ethic of Ninomiya Sontoku to build a modern nation. By late Meiji and Taishō such dreams of mass unity behind positive goals had faded: mere consciousness of growing national power was no longer enough to produce consensus and unity. Yoshimoto never clearly stated what he meant by this unity, but it was clear that in Taishō and early Shōwa a general decline in "authenticity" of feeling had set in. Nationalism was preempted by rightists like Kita Ikki and by military men and bureaucrats. As evidence of the change in feeling he cited changes in the lyrics of popular songs after World War I. Songs of the 1920s were marked by a new sadness: they were full of such words as "abandon," "cut," "cry," "go back," "forget," "cannot return," and the like, negative words and expressions that symbolized emotions of hardening and decline. Such lyrics were not mere sentimentality, but reflected a sad awareness on "the people's" part that capitalism had turned manipulative and that they as well as the intellectuals were being exploited. And he maintained that such feelings had carried over into the postwar period.[61]

By 1964 Yoshimoto had lost whatever interest he had ever had in the organized leftwing political movement. Japanese capitalism had found its opponents only too easy to deal with: leftist ideology had never attracted more than a small fragment of the culture. The left offered the dogmas of international socialism, abstractions which might reach a minority of students and urban intellectuals but which could not hope to move a whole people. On the right were images of love, folk-experience, instinct, concreteness, *minzoku*-type symbols, all equally abused and betrayed by the national leaders. Thus "internationalism" of the left and "ultranationalism" of the right were both to blame for crimes against "the people."[62]

Yoshimoto felt that he owed a debt to European utopian thought but none whatever to the Japanese "social movement." His task and that of his contemporaries, who had endured the disasters of war at their most impressionable age, was to develop their own ideas about self and nation. But how was this to be done? Like many others in his easy acceptance of Marxian categories, he had drifted into the anti-treaty movement in the late 1950s only to be deeply shocked by the spectacle of the Communist Party's manipulative tactics and anti-revolutionary behavior during the treaty crisis. Knowing and caring less about power politics than about ideas, language and culture, Yoshimoto condemned the communists after 1960 and attacked both left and right for their abandonment of the cause of "the people."[63] He clearly saw that much of the left's hostility toward the United States after the war was little more than prewar xenophobia in new dress. But what truly obsessed him from about 1964 on was how intellectuals of whatever stripe were to relate to "the people," and how the true weight of popular feeling and belief was to bring itself to bear in the formation of new intellectual rationalizations of Japanese history.

He struggled to put what he meant into words:

> Throughout life the people cannot be separated from the home and workplace that together make their sphere of living; nor do they wish to be separated. They will live and die by giving way diffidently, without awareness, even, in the face of whatever control. If here precisely is the core of "mass nationalism," then this is worth turning into thought, as something that exists much more importantly than any politician. Here is the basis of "independence."[64]

He denied that the feelings of "the people" had so far been incorporated in any significant way in the interpretation of modern Japanese history, and he took issue with all current intellectual formulations of that history as being incomplete and inadequate. He felt that the "pragmatism" of such contemporaries as Tsurumi Shunsuke took the life and thought of "the people" too little into account.[65] And he rejected the post-Stalinist developments in international Marxism along with pragmatism:

> However thinkers and political forces of Stalinist lineage (Khrushchev, Togliatti, Mao Tse-tung and other progressive elements) conceive the future of world history within the framework of peaceful coexistence or peaceful competition, such conceptions are *ipso facto* absurd; they can never control the future of world history without nuclear war against capitalism. I deny this noth-

ingness equally as I deny the nothingness of the capitalist
system. *Mine is the standpoint of nativistic mass nationalism.*[66]

Likewise he disputed the modernization theories of such writers as Katō Shūichi or Ueyama Shumpei, who saw Japan as a
more or less successful blend of Japanese and Western elements, and put forward his own prescription for a brand of
ideas about the culture that would stress the thought of "the
people":

> Postwar nationalism of the masses . . . by being robbed at its
> base in the rural villages by the capitalist system, was turned
> into apathy as far as ideas were concerned. Mass nationalism
> since Meiji has lost any concept of itself; the nation in actuality
> no longer exists. Therefore there can be no fusion of mass
> nationalism with the capitalist state as desired by modernist
> intellectuals such as Ueyama Shumpei; nor can there be any
> absorption of mass nationalism into the internationalism of intel-
> lectuals following on the breakup of Stalinism since Stalin's
> death. Just as before, mass nationalism in Japan is the reverse
> side of the mirror of Japanese capitalism, which exists with the
> Imperial family living like a ghost in its shadow. Mass national-
> ism shows its own mirror to the ruling class, with its passion for
> peep shows and its respect for the directors of companies and
> its vague yearnings and feelings for nature and its symbols of
> popularity. The way to naturalize this mass nationalism politi-
> cally is to drive the capitalist class itself into a corner and push
> it over the edge, and in the realm of ideas, the masses them-
> selves, by deepening their living thought and making it more
> independent, will cause themselves to become more separate.
> Then both images will be turned upside down: the image of the
> citizens' [*shimin*] unification according to the nationalism as
> defined by postwar intellectuals, and the image of false socialism
> as defined by the postwar "internationalists." This idea can be
> called "independence"; but it is not a matter of name but of
> reality. To walk without compromise will be long and difficult.[67]

As his ideas about "independence" were elaborated in the
late 1960s, Yoshimoto came to understand ultranationalism not
merely as a reactionary political phenomenon that would nec-

essarily be removed as Japanese society grew more modern and by implication more like the West, but rather as the product of religious sentiments that long antedated and in fact brought about the formation of law and the state itself. Arguing as the Marxists had done that Japan was pushed into ultranationalism by the Western colonial powers was as superficial as arguing that Russia after 1917 was pushed into building a socialist state by the Western imperialists. Such conditions may have been necessary but they were not sufficient to explain what happened.[68] The debate on nationalism in Japan had for Yoshimoto touched on only the more superficial socioeconomic or political-structural aspects of the problem and in many respects had reduced itself to a matter of temperamental differences among the disputants. Hence his quarrel with Maruyama; whereas the problem as he saw it by the late 1960s was basically religious and ethical, and went to the roots of Japanese sentiment about the emperor and the natural world. To him what was vital was not so much the distortions that attended the expansion of the means of production as the real meaning of the expansion of the people's "illusion" of common ethical and religious feeling. And he compared Japanese ultranationalism with Christian socialism in the 19th-century West.[69]

Thus as the postmortems of the Security Treaty crisis continued over the following decade, Yoshimoto found himself locked in a vigorous debate with some of the most distinguished intellectuals of his time. In the process he increasingly took a nativistic (*dochaku*) position, insisting that ideas of "independence" and Japanese nationality sprang from the deepest religio-ethical-mythological roots; that they derived ultimately from prehistoric popular illusions and shibboleths about the emperor-ruler, and that such ideas could not be regarded as pathological but possessed all the power of the illusions of any primitive nature-religion. Herein lay the flaw in the orthodox Marxist interpretation of Japanese society, which had never really faced the problem of religion as a formative element in the growth of the state but instead saw Japan in narrow terms as a "social state," the product of

secular economic and social forces. This missed the nature of
Japanese despotism, in which the state grew out of laws that
in turn had been produced by the religious sentiments of the
kyōdōtai.[70]

Furthermore, Yoshimoto now came to believe that in order
for intellectuals ever to comprehend how distant "the people"
were from the intellectuals' conception of them, their language
would have to be studied much more carefully, and the differences between the language of the "vanguard" or intellectual
elite and the "folk" would have to be more fully analyzed and
understood. Nationalism in Japan was not just a matter of
"progressive" versus "reactionary" or "fascism" versus "democracy"; nationalism meant probing in the memory of "the
people" for elemental language and ideas, or what he called
"language thought" *(gengo shisō)*, and trying to bring these to
the surface and somehow to fuse them with the language and
ideas of the "vanguard." In this respect, he believed that the
work of the ethnologist, Yanagita Kunio, and his school, while
it had a certain value, had ultimately failed: despite their
collection of vast amounts of antiquarian data bearing on
popular beliefs, this material still had not been incorporated in
the consciousness of the elite and put to full use.

In his effort to express himself he fell again and again into
obscurity; at times he seemed to extol the non-verbal and
intuitive mode;[71] but at base he felt a conviction that "the
people" needed to be better understood and included in the
intellectuals' perception of the national life, if Japanese national or cultural identity as a whole was ever to be clearly
defined. Ironically, the more he explored relationships with
"the people," the more he wrote about them in a highly
complex, allusive, and obscure language that most of them
would have had great difficulty understanding, even had they
read it. Yet he argued with increasing shrillness that unless
intellectuals of both Marxist and "pragmatist" persuasions
stopped neglecting how "the people" felt and spoke and
expressed themselves, they would never understand the *real*
nature of Japanese nationalism or grasp the "ideological basis
of independence" which was the object of his critical search.

For just as the state began in religion and other "generalized concepts" such as law, so language had an "inner essence" of self-expressiveness entirely different from its "outer essence" of communication or designation of meaning.[72]

The size of Yoshimoto's audience was hard to estimate, but he attracted a growing following among younger intellectuals and students, and his many books could be found in abundance on the shelves of Tokyo bookstores. As the 1960s passed, he continued to show little concern for the public causes that drew support from many other intellectuals: he regarded the "movements" against the Vietnam War and nuclear testing as futile expressions of frustration felt by those who could do nothing to change national policy and who lived in a country that could produce neither peace nor war. Such movements were led by what he called "reviewing-stand intellectuals," who cheered on the fighting people of Vietnam and talked foolishly about peace, just as they had talked about victory at the time of the Security Treaty crisis. Some of these writings had a very bitter tone: America, China, and the USSR all were coldly realistic about Vietnam, but never Japan's intellectuals, those romantics trapped between peace and war; and he excoriated war reporters and others who felt that they had to go to Vietnam to find death, when death was obvious in the Japanese intellectuals' suspension between war and peace—those intellectuals who had never had an original idea but went on endlessly producing disciples.[73] Meanwhile, he asserted, intellectual stereotypes of "the people" persisted: they must love peace, oppose war, protest against authority, and so on. Yet the intellectuals themselves lived in a closed world of intellection, without basic connection with the world of "the people's" feeling or language, and taken in by the "common illusion" of the state, which enclosed all. By contrast, he praised the student movement above other "artifically maintained manifestations" of unrest such as the peace and anti-bomb movements; and he was briefly prominent as an intellectual leader of students during the university disturbances in Tokyo in 1968 and 1969.[74]

Professor Tsurumi Kazuko noted that students belonging to

the Zenkyōtō faction of Zengakuren took up Yoshimoto's term *jiritsu,* or "independence," and used it in various meanings during their demonstrations against the university authorities. Tsurumi pointed out that in his 1964 essay on nationalism (see above) Yoshimoto had defined this term as

> the nationalism of the common man, claiming that common indigenous ways of thinking as distinguished from those of the elite had never been given due consideration in Japanese intellectual history and asserting that he would himself therefore be responsible for interpreting the ideas and feelings of the masses. Accordingly, in his [Yoshimoto's] context *jiritsu* meant a quest for an indigenous pattern of thinking that could be universalized not only as an instrument of interpretation but also as an instrument of change. He called his application the nationalism of the common man, because it repudiated all exogenous means that would analyze and change Japanese society.[75]

According to Tsurumi, the emphasis in Yoshimoto's concept of *jiritsu* upon the common man

> differs considerably from the emphasis of the Communist Party upon a class-conscious proletariat. By "common men," Yoshimoto meant those who would not and could not leave the sphere of their daily lives that lies between their homes and workplaces, and who live and die indifferent to whatever political rule they are placed under.[76]

She also noted that Yoshimoto's *jiritsu* concept had taken on an existential orientation among students, "whose individual reference is selfhood and whose group reference is humanity as a whole"; and that

> among the leaders of the anti-Communist Party factions [of Zengakuren] *jiritsu* has taken on political implication through which those national groups fighting native imperialism may eventually achieve the solidarity of an international revolutionary cause.[77]

In this respect, if in no other, Yoshimoto's ideas may have had some impact on the political scene. Such notions of independence may indeed have fired some students to protest. Yet there was nowhere in his writings any clear prescription by which he proposed to energize the people through ideas of *jiritsu* to promote political change; and it could be argued that, in spite of his desire to "push the capitalists over the edge," his ideas of "independence" were more closely related to ethical or psychological concerns than to any political program, and may even had made the revolution more remote by refocusing attention on internal, non-economic goals.

III

In his book on indigenous and imported thought, Ueyama Shumpei applied to Yoshimoto what Yoshimoto once wrote about Akutagawa Ryūnosuke, i.e., that he was trapped in his self-hatred, his inferiority complexes and social origins, and could not become a "great intellectual"; hence Yoshimoto's envy and resentment of Maruyama Masao.[78] Ueyama placed Yoshimoto in the same line with Shinran, Motoori Norinaga, Itō Jinsai, Origuchi Shinobu and Yanagita Kunio, "all distinguished by their capacity to attract passionate feeling," and he offered the following summation of Yoshimoto's significance in the history of postwar Japanese thought:

In the natural philosophy of the School of National Learning, Yoshimoto found the core of Japanese nationalism. By natural philosophy Yoshimoto meant the whole tradition of natural ideas from their simplest biological and botanical expressions up to the notion of the "emperor-system." The idea of "nature" and the "natural" was the "dynamic image" that held this whole native intellectual tradition together. Yet he realized that both ends of the ladder of traditional nationalistic feeling had become fatally attenuated after the war: the farmers at the bottom had been turned into capitalist entrepreneurs, while the unifying efficacy of the Emperor had been lost. In Yoshimoto's words, the points of the compass of nationalism have swung from a vertical to a horizontal axis since the war. And so the core of nationalism can only be in the people's horizontally dispersed existence.

And Ueyama continued:

[Erwin] Baelz, who came to Japan in the early years of Meiji, heard Japanese say about their own history, "we are barbarians," or "we have no history, our history begins now." The same kind of thing was heard after the defeat in 1945. The theories of Maruyama are the most refined, scholarly variation of such ideas. By denying Japan's past and setting up an idealized foreign past as the goal of Japan's future, such theories look like internationalism; but in that they arise from an overflowing patriotism and represent a reappearance of a very old tradition of self-denying receptivity toward advanced civilizations, national qualities clearly lie behind them. By contrast, when Yoshimoto with quite unfitting bravado says that there is nothing whatever to be learned from foreign countries, this makes a very nationalistic impression at first hearing, but something in this whole idea goes against the feeling in the mainstream of Japanese tradition. However, when Buddhism had become a puppet in Japanese hands, Shinran appeared; when neo-Confucianism had become a puppet in Japanese hands, Jinsai appeared. In Shinran's time the doctrines of Shintō were newly elaborated; in Jinsai's time the same was true of National Learning, and from the lineage of *kokugaku* and Shintō came Yanagita and Origuchi. If we bear all this in mind, if we remember that Yoshimoto once wrote that "the only men I recognize as experts in a certain field are Origuchi and Yanagita," that he preferred Jinsai to Sorai, and wrote that "the meaning of the modern Confucianism of Sokō and Jinsai is very close to the medieval temple-thought of Hōnen and Shinran," then one can see that the feeling that supports his theories is conspicuously nationalistic. . . . Jinsai stood against Confucianism, Shinran against Buddhism; just so, Yoshimoto modelled his own position on theirs, stood against the "vanguard" thought of today's world and took up the position of what he called "independence." In this was the basis of his nationalism. . . . As against Maruyama, who went beyond Fukuzawa's political rejection of Asia and advocated spiritual rejection as well, Yoshimoto took up his *dochaku* position: we cannot separate ourselves from the living sphere that is connected with our own occupation, our family, nor should we try. Against the substance of the world's vanguard thought, he answered with this *dochaku* language.[79]

Asked to react to this description of his position, Yoshimoto compared it to a coffin into which he could be fit if he must be.[80] Yet, while the lineage Ueyama proposed for Yoshimoto was itself quite diverse, on the whole Ueyama's comments seemed apt. Yoshimoto's stress on "the people" as a kind of poetic, vitalistic entity, whose daily life and "thought" were endowed with affective qualities of at least implied virtue, did not spring primarily from mere antiquarian tendencies or nostalgia for lost agrarian verities. On one level he needed the idea of "the people" as a kind of anti-elite to reify his own elitist existence. On another level, his yearning for them stemmed from a massive sense of personal and national loss after 1945. Because he identified most naturally with those Japanese intellectuals who were least representative of the *Keimōsha* (Enlightener) tradition, he spoke with some approval of Yanagita and especially of Origuchi, who, he thought, had grasped the "unchanging idea of community" throughout Japanese history. But Yoshimoto's "people" were not entirely subsumed in the term *dochaku,* if that term was taken merely as a metaphor drawn from agricultural society. He knew well enough that the idea of community had become profoundly attenuated, yet he believed that to some degree it still existed and still drew emotion toward it; and what was most essential, in his view, was to hold up the idea of ordinary people with ordinary experiences as integral to the mental history of an ongoing Japanese society, not just as a problem for academic research governed by Western-originated methodologies, nor as a repository of some archaic "authentic" uniqueness of the folk.[81]

By "the people" he meant those Japanese who thought only of their daily lives and profit, who were not concerned with events beyond the sphere of their *nichijō seikatsu* (everyday life), and who were not involved in the process of thinking about their times. The purpose of the intellectuals' vocation, he thought, was to think about "the people," to "materialize and deepen intellectuals' thinking about the people's lives."[82] This function the intellectuals must perform outside any party framework; nor should they be forced into periods of labor in the countryside to improve their understanding of "the people's" lives. Rather, they should strive, free from party control, to "put their hands out to the people."

He nowhere explained more clearly how this was to be done. Rather one felt that, by design, his "people" remained metaphysical to a degree, more idea than reality, or, rather, seen by him to be more real as idea than as fact. This tendency to idealize them, which Yoshimoto readily admitted, was attributed by Maruyama to Yoshimoto's literary vocation as well as to his despair over the masses in defeat in 1945.[83] With no personal experience of the evolution of prewar thought, Yoshimoto's own intellectual pilgrimage had taken him from conventional chauvinism to a shocked desire to identify, not with a class-conscious proletariat but with a romantic image of the masses. Certainly his "people" were in no sense liberal *shimin,* "new citizens" with a growing sense of such a concept. But neither were they primarily farmers or fishermen. When asked to explain who they were, he could only repeat: those who thought only of their daily round of existence. Yet, though his "people" may have had no concrete political consequence, he could not let them go, could not, like Takeuchi Yoshimi, see the intellectual's true vocation to lie on the margins of the productive society, could not feel, as Takeuchi did, that the intellectual's mission was to complete his separation from the people.[84]

In Yoshimoto one had a type of intellectual or man of letters common in Japan and Europe but much less so in the United States. While his earliest affiliations were literary, the bulk of his writings lay not in works of the imagination but in the critical essay form. His *zenshū* in fifteen volumes ranged from lyric poetry through essays on the war responsibility of writers, to mass nationalism, and disquisitions on linguistics, esthetics, existential phenomenology, medieval Japanese poetry, color spectra, and the southern origins of the Japanese people.

While he was ready to admit to a lack of expertise in many fields, this never prevented him from writing about any of them he chose. He saw himself as a freelance critic of whatever struck his fancy, and from the early postwar period onward he had little difficulty in finding an outlet in print for whatever he wished to say. From 1964 he was the sole editor of the journal, *Shikō,* which he founded in 1961 along with the poet Tanikawa Gan, and others, and which served as a vehicle for his ideas. In 1970 he finally quit his job in the licensing office and thereafter supported himself through his writings.

Yoshimoto's career could be viewed as determined largely by two events, both of them defeats, in August 1945 and May–June 1960. The Emperor's broadcast destroyed the world of his boyhood beliefs and left him with permanent scorn for the older generation, whom he saw as the prime source of his betrayal. He especially rejected intellectuals older than himself, projecting upon them much of the disillusionment he felt after 1945. Embarked in the 1950s onto a sea of polemics about intellectuals and "the people," nationalism, the "situation," and so on, he often seemed as much enclosed in a glass paperweight world of intellection as those whom he attacked, caught up in disputes about modernization or illusion. Yet he did not appear to be concerned, in his eagerness to demolish his intellectual opponents, that they took him to task for a lack of objectivity and a certain narcissism. Rather he seemed confident that his thought would inevitably be an influence over events, because by definition it was more real than any events.

How to measure his influence remained uncertain, although evidence of his intellectual force and charismatic personality was reflected in the strong reactions of many of his contemporaries to his writings, and the admiration of his coterie of followers. In any event, there was something poignant in Yoshimoto's anti-scientific groping for an "inner world" of the people's sentiments, their expressive language and their songs, just as there was something deeply meaningful, to him, if vaguely troubling, to others, about his locating their "independence" somewhere in the imprecise area of the emotions, in the affirmation of patterns of undelineated feelings of "ordinary" Japanese. They were what he chose to use, to hold up anyhow against what he regarded as the insidiousness of alien methodologies as well as to employ as a caution against the reappearance, however far-fetched that might seem, of the perversities of a dismantled past.

1978

CHAPTER FOUR

Tsurumi Shunsuke in Two Worlds

This essay on the career and major writings of Tsurumi Shunsuke explores the question of cross-cultural debt and disillusionment as illustrated in the life of one prominent upper middle-class Japanese intellectual noted for his repeated protests against the centers of power in his society after 1945 as well as against what he perceived to be American departure from goals and ideals that had inspired him as a student in New England before the Second World War. If most Japanese intellectuals could be seen drawing their primary nourishment from one of three main sources—the West, China, or the Japanese past—then in Tsurumi one felt the force of Western—in his case, American—ideas in their purest form. Enrolled in a Massachusetts preparatory school in 1938 and a 1942 graduate of Harvard College, he imbibed American literature and philosophy from teachers who were themselves pupils of great figures of the late 19th and early 20th century, men like William James, Charles Sanders Peirce, and George Herbert Mead. America was thus permanently associated in his mind with the founders of classical pragmatism as well as with such earlier writers as Emerson, Thoreau, Whitman, Melville and Hawthorne. Against such larger-than-life figures Tsurumi would later measure American embroilment in the Vietnam War and the American alliance with conservative Japanese leaders seen as more or less tarred with the brush of collaboration with the military before 1945.

Tsurumi's career provided an example of the modern Japanese intellectual's chronic problem of "teleological insight," defined by Robert Scalapino as the "*assumed* capacity to discern the future of one's own society by projecting it in accordance with conditions and trends" in the "advanced" West.[1] Held tightly between nostalgia for the solidarities of their own society's pre-modern past, with all its virtue and dubiety, and the pressure of ideas and ideals imported from an irresistible but alien Western world, postwar Japanese intellectuals in their writings often seemed to the foreign observer to be on the verge of dissolution in a terrain of attenuation and nuance, unable to resolve the meaning of their nationality.

Yet an exploration of Tsurumi's mental life, as of that of his generation after 1945, did yield some consistent themes: an ironic yearning for union with the "common people"; a wish for a way to balance thinking with acting; a need to work through the whole problem of war responsibility; a need, above all, to find something usable in the Japanese tradition while not letting go of what had been proven good in Western thought, including its perceived clarity of expression. For to Tsurumi, at least, it was not enough for intellectuals to fashion some abstract synthesis of native and Western ways of thinking and behaving; they had to enunciate this synthesis in a manner that would help create whatever consensus might be possible to overcome the social and emotional forces that still kept Japanese apart from one another as well as from other peoples. Surely some such romantic ideal lay behind the unremitting writing activity of Tsurumi and his intellectual peers in the years after 1945.

On one level Tsurumi was a classic case of an intellectual rebel out of sympathy with the main drift of the society of his birth and full of distress at the direction of his adoptive intellectual home; his hostility toward postwar America was exceeded only by his antagonism toward Japan's own leaders, and his feelings toward both were shown in a series of actions. On another level, however, he sought throughout his career as a social critic and teacher of philosophy for a union of Western knowledge with Japanese inspiration about how to live. His career in protest, while more flamboyant and provocative than his writings on culture, was in the end less significant than his search for a formulation of the peculiar distinctiveness of Japanese national and personal life after 1945 that could be put clearly into words and that might enlighten all about what it meant to be a Japanese in the late 20th century.

I

Tsurumi Shunsuke, the second of four children and an eldest son, was born in Sangenjaya, Tokyo, in 1922. His father, Yūsuke, came from modest origins in Okayama Prefecture, graduated from Tokyo Imperial University and began his career in the Railways Ministry. In 1924, after passage of the new immigration law by the American Congress, Yūsuke left the Railways Ministry and spent much of his time in the United States, where he undertook to help counteract anti-Japanese feeling as a lobbyist for Japan's cause. A delegate to the periodic conferences of the Institute of Pacific Relations, he travelled and spoke widely in America, where he was remembered in 1984 by one who had known him as "courtly and charming" and where he made influential friends.[2] He published several books, including two novels,[3] and from 1928 on was elected repeatedly to the Lower House of the Diet. After World War II Yūsuke was purged but in 1950 was rehabilitated and elected to the Upper House as a member of the *Shimpōtō* wing of the conservative political establishment. He served as Minister of Health in the Hatoyama Cabinet in the mid-1950s.

In Shunsuke's childhood, when the family never seemed to have a lasting living-place—they moved ten times before the boy reached sixth grade[4]—he came to regard his father as a buffer between himself and his difficult mother, and it was the father's retreat in the Shinshū mountains rather than any of their numerous houses, which he recalled with nostalgia many years later.[5] At least Yūsuke was not a scold. When in the late

1930s he showed signs of growing sympathy for the militarists, his son remembered thinking it odd, but his father's partiality toward him remained firmly in his memory.[6]

His mother was a different sort. From samurai stock on both sides, she was the daughter of Gotō Shimpei, archetypal Meiji bureaucrat and intimate of the leaders of Victorian Japan. Gotō had been deeply involved in the whole modernizing enterprise: a physician, he organized the sanitation bureau in the Home Ministry and later was civil governor of the new colony of Taiwan, head of the South Manchurian Railway Company, and a member of several Cabinets. In 1920 he became mayor of Tokyo, and as Home Minister played a central role in the rebuilding of the city after the 1923 earthquake.[7] A man of formidable energies, Gotō overawed his daughter and left her with an ineradicable sense of her own insignificance and worthlessness; her marriage to a minor bureaucrat in the Railways Ministry, which her father had run at one point in his career, only increased her self-mortifying tendencies.[8] Loving her eldest son to the point of suffocation, she instilled in him her self-hatred, and even as a child his instinctive awareness of what she was doing to him produced a fierce rection: "To me, my mother was a formidable enemy, always commanding my respect, even when I fought her tooth and nail."[9] To him, her endless service to her husband and his numerous relatives also sprang from an abnormal sense of shame and self-hatred, which he thought might help to account for his own "erratic behavior from my childhood to this day."[10]

If as an adult Shunsuke realized that his mother had had a low opinion of herself and had taught him to behave in the same way, in his early childhood fear of being scolded by her brought on the behavior most likely to produce the feared result. He stole cakes and ate them and was upbraided when caught. His mother was given to exclaiming that "because it is my responsibility for having such a child, we will stab each other and die!"[11] Not surprisingly, such dramatics panicked the boy and made his life generally miserable. She scolded him for making paper airplanes, for taking three hours to get home from school, for being involved in a shoplifting incident. At least once he was put into a mental clinic operated by a relative, but, he lamented, because his mother went with him to the clinic, he did not improve.[12] According to his own account, two other visits to mental institutions were connected with failed suicide attempts.[13]

Oppressed and insulted by his mother's smothering attentions, Tsurumi came to equate love with being monopolized and manipulated. Later he felt that his mother had interposed herself between him and the objects of his sexual desire; happiness became an escape from her neuroses, her aversion to natural human functions, her fear of dirt and her shame over his feelings.[14] And beyond whatever guilty fears his mother instilled in him, he soon came to identify her with the Meiji world she derived from and to abhor its embrace of progress, its notion of "must do, therefore can do," that admitted to no possibility of failure and that, he thought, lay behind the breakdown in the relation between man and nature in modern Japanese life. By the late 1960s, after she was dead, he could afford to feel some nostalgia over the hell of their daily struggles,[15] but he never forgave her for bequeathing to him a mistaken idea of love. He was unable to show much sympathy for her conversion to Christianity in the 1930s, when, blaming herself for her lack of "sincerity," she "begged the forgiveness of God."[16]

Tsurumi graduated from primary school in 1935, but his Japanese education was already nearly at an end. After being withdrawn, or expelled, from two middle schools, he suffered a period of acute depression. Writing much later, he noted that some of his teachers in this period had been brought up in the era of "Taishō democracy" and believed that Japanese should not give way to chauvinism and xenophobia but should remain open to each other and the world.[17] At this stage he read a version of the autobiography of Booker T. Washington translated by his school's principal, but in general he was silent about this period of his youth. According to his biographer,

> In his middle school days Kropotkin's autobiography intrigued him, not so much because he could deny the state directly

through Kropotkin as that in Kropotkin he read of a negative
that stood at the opposite pole from the authority represented
by his mother. Here was located an internal support for the
thoroughgoing denial of authority in [Tsurumi's] anarchism.[18]

In 1938, seeking some way to deal with his increasingly
recalcitrant son, Yūsuke sent him briefly to Australia.[19] When
for whatever reason that experiment failed, the father took
advantage of one of his American connections and wrote to
Professor Arthur Schlesinger, Sr., of the Harvard History
Department, about gaining admission to an American preparatory school. Schlesinger had visited the Tsurumi family some
years earlier in Japan, and Shunsuke, on a brief visit to the
United States in 1937, had stayed with the Schlesingers in
Cambridge and visited the Belmont Hill School. Now Professor Schlesinger contacted the headmaster of the Middlesex
School in Concord, Massachusetts, and arrangements were
soon made to admit the young Tsurumi as a special student,
with the possibility that he might be able to enter Harvard
after one year.[20] In the preliminary correspondence Tsurumi
Yūsuke was identified as a liberal and a friend of the then
Prime Minister, Konoe Fumimaro.

Middlesex was a boarding school for boys with an enroll-
ment of about one hundred, set in the countryside of Thoreau,
Emerson and Hawthorne. To Tsurumi, arriving with his father
on the day of the great September 1938 hurricane, it must have
seemed a strange world; many years later he recalled the daily
prayers, the hymn-singing and Bible-reading, the black suits
and white shirts with neckties that the boys wore to chapel.
He associated Concord and the school with the Puritans. Boys
who committed "careless" offenses, such as tardiness, unti-
diness, and the like, were awarded demerits and had to run
around the grounds, four or five "rounds" to a mile; by the
end of the year Tsurumi had set some kind of record for
"rounds" performed. In the winter, when he was put in the
school infirmary with influenza, he noticed that the middle-
aged nurses used euphemisms to refer to bodily functions and
were incomprehensible to him much of the time.[21]

He was totally alone, the only foreign student in the school, in special circumstances and not associated formally with any class. A few students sought him out, at least one of these chance meetings resulting in a lifelong friendship.[22] School officials and faculty were solicitous and extended themselves to show care and concern for the new Japanese boy; yet for weeks and months he had trouble understanding his teachers and they him. As one of them recalled in 1984:

> The problem with this remarkable, bespectacled little boy was to place him in classes he could handle. He had had enough math to meet college requirements, but his spoken English was limited to some very polite comments, said with a smile. His reading ability was fairly well advanced, but one was never sure at the beginning whether he understood what was said to him. He usually answered, "Yes, sir" to everything.[23]

The same teacher recalled Tsurumi's study habits and revealed something of how life went on from day to day between students and teachers:

> [Mr. Tsurumi] asked me to try hard to persuade his son not to study too hard but to get some daily exercise. I found out fairly soon what a difficult task this was. Shunsuke slept in a room with a desk and a bookcase. Every night I came in to persuade him that it was bedtime. He begged for permission to stay up longer. His self-imposed routine for the late hours was to make a list of the articles around him, the words he had not understood during the day, etc. . . . . He learned them, fifty every evening, after looking them up in his Japanese dictionary.[24]

The correspondence between school officials and Tsurumi's father, who was then staying at the Plaza Hotel in New York City, was filled with hope and discouragement: though his teachers found it hard to know how to grade papers that were at first unreadable, they were certain that he would persevere and improve. Whether the careful treatment they gave him was unusual is uncertain; probably it was not, but in any case, with work and good intentions all round, Tsurumi's English improved rapidly, and by mid-term he was holding his own in English composition and in American and European history classes. Meanwhile Harvard was keeping watch and was prepared to let him take the College Board examinations in these three subjects (later reduced to two) and to give him credit for his native Japanese.

Tsurumi's year at Middlesex School was a central experience of his life. He never thought of the place without pleasure. Friendships made there endured when disaffection with most other things, American and Japanese, accumulated. Life at school was not all study: on weekends he would walk in to Concord, two miles each way, to drink Coca-Cola at the local drugstore.[25] One teacher recalled:

> As for exercise, we had no thought of football. He spent some happy afternoons out in our woods and down by the pond. The Japanese gardens he concocted to give to Mrs. Terry and the other ladies of the faculty were made in baking tins or big bowls lent for the purpose; they were a joy to see.[26]

Nearly fifty years later one classmate remembered the "box gardens" and confirmed that Tsurumi's standing with the other boys was always good.[27] Tsurumi himself noted that making miniature gardens had been a kind of psychological therapy for him.[28]

In the summer of 1939 Tsurumi passed the College Board examinations, received his certificate of course completion from Middlesex and was admitted to Harvard. The school's influence followed him to Cambridge; before leaving Concord he had been introduced to the family of Mrs. Kenneth T. Young, of Chauncy Street, Cambridge, and after a trial period in the summer, arrangements were made for him to live with the Youngs during the regular academic year. This was remarkably fortunate for all concerned. Charles W. Young had been at Middlesex with Tsurumi, though a year behind him; and Charles' older brother, Kenneth, later to become a State Department official, had travelled in China and Japan. Mrs. Young took Tsurumi in and treated him as a family member;

she coaxed him to eat his breakfast and he waited to be coaxed: surrogate mothers were more fun than his real one. Mrs. Young's own mother furthered his English language training by having him read books in English aloud to her.[29] He remained with the Young ménage until the fall before Pearl Harbor, when he moved into separate rooms.[30]

Tsurumi's initial encounter with America was cushioned by the concern and support of his American sponsors, but success was not automatic and required all of his own efforts. When he received a failing grade on his first mid-term exam in English composition at Harvard, Mrs. Young's mother undertook to visit his instructor to acquaint him with the special problems that attended a foreign student's life; however, she had no special influence, and it was due primarily to Tsurumi's own hard work that he finished the term with a C, and the second term with a B.[31] No doubt his American experiences and the absence of Japanese ones meant that his future status in the eyes of his Japanese contemporaries would be defined in exotic terms; but if missing the experience of a college education in Japan caused him any apprehension at this time or later, he gave no signs of it. America meant first of all escape from his mother's stifling presence. Meanwhile, at Harvard if not at Middlesex he was reading Emerson, Thoreau and other writers, and their injunctions in such works as Emerson's "American Scholar" essay and Thoreau's *Walden* on how to live, on the link between thought and action, their stress on self-reliance, individualism and character-building moved him deeply. An upper bourgeois Japanese boy from a family with its roots in the Meiji governing apparatus, he seems not to have been aware of such social realities as racial discrimination in America; apparently he felt no such discrimination himself as a student, but if he did, he did not record it. Blacks, American Indians, and other minorities remained for him to discover much later at an entirely different stage of his career.

At Harvard Tsurumi enrolled in philosophy courses, and for the next two and a half years, under the direction of Professor Ralph Barton Perry, the biographer of William James, he immersed himself in the study of American philosophy. This,

among other things, meant pragmatism; and while he had
already read Kant, Hegel and other European philosophers to
some extent, now he plunged in and explored the thought of
the classical pragmatists, mainly, it appears, because "they
were there." From the first he was powerfully attracted to
William James' link between ideas and the working out of their
practical results; metaphysics interested him less than a philosophical attitude that tested and judged ideas by their usefulness. As he later quoted as a "maxim of pragmatism,"
"Thought means something that can be revealed in the form
of action."[32] At a time when in Europe Hitler was defying the
other Western powers and Spain had fallen to the Franco
forces, in Cambridge Tsurumi lived in a cocoon of philosophical speculation, moving between his rented room, the class-
room and the library, totally absorbed by his books, until the
afternoon of February 24, 1942, when three agents of the
Federal Bureau of Investigation knocked on his door at 43
Irving Street.

He wrote of this episode many times, but the details were
always pretty much the same. The FBI men came in and
professed to be intrigued with the wooden crucifix on the wall.
Why, they wanted to know, if he was an anarchist, as they
suspected, did he have a crucifix? After a lengthy search of his
room, during which he offered the agents a drink from his
bottle of milk on the window-ledge, he was arrested and taken
to a detention center of the Immigration Service in East
Boston.[33] How far his arrest was due to his political views and
how far it was a part of the general round-up of enemy aliens
after December 7, 1941 is not entirely clear.

Tsurumi remained at the detention center for several
months, in spite of the efforts of his Harvard professors to
obtain his release. His time in detention was spent mainly
working on his senior paper on "The Pragmatism of William
James," which he wrote while sitting on the floor of the
detention center toilet and using the toilet seat as a desk. This
paper was later accepted, and he was graduated with a B.S.
degree (signifying no classical languages) in the spring of 1942.
In his accounts of this period of his life he noted that no

Japanese university would have been likely to allow him to graduate in such a short time. He also noted that he was not tortured or otherwise badly treated; indeed, he seems to have had some light moments in detention, at least in retrospect. He told of writing love letters in English to the sweetheart of a fellow prisoner, a German sailor; and he compared life at the center at one point to a Marx brothers movie. Another prisoner borrowed his copy of Plato's *Republic* and read it for five days running.[34]

Eventually Tsurumi was transferred via Ellis Island to Fort Meade, Maryland and on June 10, 1942, along with his elder sister, Kazuko, and numerous other Japanese caught in the United States by the war, was put aboard the Swedish repatriation ship *Gripsholm,* to be transferred to the *Asama Maru* in Mozambique. He reached Japan on August 20, 1942; but even before the ship docked Tsurumi had had premonitions of his future life and its concerns. Once the Japanese were all alone together on the *Asama Maru,* away from Europeans or Americans, he noticed how the atmosphere suddenly changed; and he sounded a theme that was to recur in one way or another in his later writings: "Japanese society was more of a prison for me than an American prison had been."[35] As a Japanese he had not wanted to see the war end, as he thought it must, in Japan's defeat while he was absent from his home country; yet once alone among them, "my idea of greeting defeat among the Japanese seemed a kind of rash idealism."[36] Being home again brought its quota of chagrin, especially so as five days after the ship docked, he was ordered to present himself for examination for active service.

He was spared active duty for health reasons, but in early 1943 was sent to Java as a civilian employee of the navy. There he monitored Allied radio broadcasts and made up a daily "newspaper" based on their contents, which presumably resembled papers the enemy was reading and would give a more accurate account of the progress of military operations than the fictions being purveyed by Japan's Imperial General Headquarters. At least, such appeared to have been the hope of Tsurumi's superiors in Java, who were troubled by the fact

that enemy ships which Headquarters reported had been sunk
were still afloat and fighting.[37]

In Java Tsurumi continued with his bookish interests; although he was in Asia, he showed little interest in it. Instead,
he listened to T. S. Eliot lecturing on the radio on Joyce's
Finnegan's Wake; and his reading included Thomas à Kempis,
Epictetus, Marcus Aurelius, Lao Tzu, Karl Mannheim, Mali-
nowsky, Havelock Ellis (on whom he later wrote a long article)
and Schopenhauer. One wonders whether he took all these
authors to Java with him in his kit or found them in "Batavia."
Yet he was also thinking, as early as the end of 1944, of what
he might do after the war. The memory of how the cultural
atmosphere of the human group on the repatriation ship had
changed, how the Japanese had all suddenly somehow presented a cultural "front" once they were together and alone
and headed back home remained in his mind but now stimulated his desire to know more about ideological change. He
dreamed of a two-volume work on the subject; meantime, a
lung infection required two operations, and after a prolonged
stay in a Japanese naval hospital in Southeast Asia, he was
invalided to Japan in late 1944. Leaving navy work, he recu-
perated at the hot spring resort of Atami, where he heard the
Emperor's broadcast of surrender on August 15, 1945. His
principal reaction to the broadcast was that the voice was
unfamiliar and unpleasant *(bukimi),* and he thought it disgust-
ing *(iya)* that the Emperor had spoken only of the cruelty of
the enemy and had said nothing of the long, cruel war waged
by the Japanese themselves.[38]

II

In August 1945 Tsurumi was only 23 years old. He had no
peers from middle or higher school in Japan and no record of
attending a Japanese university. Virtually without friends, he
could only have been regarded as a stranger, if not a foreigner,
by other Japanese. One of a privileged few who had been
educated in the United States before the war, he was still in

rebellion against his mother's pressure to succeed in conventional ways, and he readily identified her world with the conservative politicians, bureaucrats and businessmen whom he soon saw reemerging with American encouragement to run the country after the war, and who included his own father, soon to be restored to respectability as a conservative member of the Diet. His own family's behavior thus confirmed his intellectual resentment against the powers-that-be and added to his feelings of personal guilt and responsibility for what had happened to his country:

> August 15, 1945 was a shameful incident for me and for the Japanese people, a bitter memory. . . . Was there no possibility of realizing a republican system at that time? If there was a chance and my generation failed to make it a reality, then we must bear responsibility for the heavy burden we have left to our own grandchildren.[39]

But while he felt shame for his failure to work tangibly against the Japanese government during the war, now that the war was over he could not bring himself to join the alien Occupation forces, where he might very well have been useful; on the contrary, he very soon felt an equivalent shame for the fact of Occupation itself, and the ground was laid in the late 1940s for his highly complex and often contradictory feelings about the United States:

> Two years with [the Young family] left something inside me, something that remained even after I came back to Japan during the war and lived in a country that was fighting against America. After the war, and especially in the period from the Korean War to the war in Vietnam, I shook my small weak fist at America and tried not to be overwhelmed by America . . . and I believe that this was because I felt an obligation to Americans. . . .[40]

Like some other intellectuals who had studied in America before the war, Tsurumi was surprised by the anti-communist direction of American foreign policy which soon began to reveal itself after 1945 and felt little sympathy with that policy;

his disillusionment was accordingly sharp. By his own admission, throughout the war he had secretly supported and cherished America's cause, and had "clung to a standard of values learned during my student days."[41] Yet even during the war he had predicted that "My war with America will begin when this war ends," and he listed in his wartime diary (in English, so that it could not be read by naval colleagues) the qualities he disliked most about the United States: "race snobbishness, self-satisfiedness, materialism and capitalism, spiritual uniformitarianism, disregard for other cultures."[42] To judge from his writings, none of these traits had loomed large to him in Cambridge before the war. Leaving Cambridge in 1942, he never returned to the United States; but by the late 1940s and certainly by the Korean War, his image of America had become tarnished. Apart from sponsorship of land reform and a few other measures, the Occupation seemed to him to have accomplished little, although American authorities did seem to him to be bent upon the return of reactionaries to power and a repetition of Japan's own prewar mistakes in Asia. In the process of his politicization, a new world view emerged. Tendencies that he had associated with his own society before and during the war were now transferred to America, where they were somehow worse because they marked a gross falling off from ideals of individual freedom, direct democracy and high personal character that he had found so powerfully expressed and so appealing in American writers during his student days. Many Americans, too, might have felt such a falling off but, unlike them, Tsurumi did not have to live in America and face the task of making those ideals work under the changed conditions of late 20th-century democratic capitalism.

Increasingly, in his writings about America the country grew strangely abstract, terrainless, almost without people, a place of corrupted ideals that was bound to fail him and leave feelings of self-loathing and depression in such a scrupulous and super-sensitive spirit. His America by 1950 had become to a large extent an unchanging illusion. It was no accident that at the same time that Tsurumi was discovering the Occupation's "dark side," he was attracted by Takeuchi Yoshimi's romantic vision of China as filtered through the moral satires of the writer Lu Xun:

> [In the late 1940s] I was unable to hold up my head because of my inaction during the war; and I also felt shame that the ideals I had entrusted to the United States during the war were destroyed during the Occupation. . . . Lu Xun's method in such stories as "Ah Q" empowered me to think about my wounds; this was a conversion for me, who had always thought ideas came only from books.[43]

Reading Lu Xun, he "found how narrow [America] was within me."[44] Yet the West, not China, was what he knew; and if his scorn of American actions and policies in the world was deep, his impatience with Japanese for not thinking and expressing themselves more like Americans formed its ironic counterpart. He did not seem able to explain Occupation policies by reference to 19th-century New England character; one seemed admirable, the other contemptible. Yet even as his prejudices about America hardened, his earliest postwar writings took off from an alarmed conviction that Japan had failed to prevent militarism from developing in the 1930s, and that to avoid repetition of such a devastating error, Japanese popular culture must be explored and understood by intellectuals and some means of communication found to open up mass society and bring the life and ideas of the common man into the light of serious intellectual concern. To do this, to create a kind of May 4th Movement in Japan, could only mean using Western methodologies, since their rejection by the prewar generation had, Tsurumi thought, led to catastrophe, moral and political.

Tsurumi's exposure to pragmatism and empirical methods of research at Harvard in the 1930s had equipped him to become a leader in the postwar exploration of Japanese popular culture. In one of his earliest published articles, written before war's end, he sought to identify a sphere of "philosophical" experience in the lives of all men, common and uncommon alike. Philosophy was not just for professional academics, but must reveal a sympathy for ordinary men and women.[45] At this period Tsurumi like many others was still thinking of revolutionary change for Japan; although he wrote little explicitly about the emperor, the end of the imperial system was implied in what he wrote.

In other of his articles of this same period, linguistic reform was a primary concern. Abolition of Chinese characters and a shift to romanization of the language was being discussed with Occupation encouragement. Tsurumi attacked the philological ambiguities of academic scholarship and stressed the notorious difficulties of communication in academic Sino-Japanese. The notion that the mere mechanical accumulation of characters could more fully render meaning was, he argued, an illusion that had been nourished by prewar teachers and must be eradicated; somehow, linguistic clarity had to be achieved if another massive self-deception was to be avoided. The style and tone of such articles was hortatory; his distaste for American policies ran parallel with his urging of a rationalistic, reformist approach to problems of language.[46] Another early postwar article consisted of an exposé of the Japanese fondness for slogans and "talismanic" phrases that used language not primarily for referential purposes but as a pseudo-magical vehicle for enforcing ideas: words like *kokutai,* for instance, meant nothing rational but sent a patriotic signal along Japanese nerves.[47] Something had to be done, Tsurumi thought, about the big lies of Japanese propaganda, the way in which, for example, the media for years had talked about "liberating" Asia while concrete Japanese behavior toward other Asians had often been less than liberating.[48]

The desire to change Japanese ways of thinking, to bring "thought" into touch with everyday life, so characteristic of his early postwar years, was summed up in Tsurumi's first substantial written work, *American Philosophy (Amerika Tetsugaku),* published in 1950, a book squarely in the "enlightenment" tradition. In it, he introduced pragmatism to Japanese readers through the careers of its chief founders, whose lives and writings he summarized. Beginning with C. S. Peirce, he praised Peirce's logic while deploring the obscurities of his style and not omitting to report that Peirce seemed to have had a high opinion of the talents of Japanese for logical thought.[49] From Peirce he moved to William James, whose graceful style charmed him as it had so many others. Americans seemed able to seize meaning quickly; if only the Japanese would define their terms and communicate so readily! But beyond matters of style, in James Tsurumi thought he saw a vision of individualistic hope and openness, a resourceful optimism that taught that each man could come to grips with his potential in action.[50] This, he believed, was where Japanese "thought" had failed. Elsewhere Tsurumi praised G. H. Mead's insistence that man's basic nature was not yet settled; indeed, what endeared American pragmatism to him was its insistence on the importance of process, its doubting any way of thinking that fixed man's nature, his *honshitsu,* its questioning of the validity of all "systems."[51] Tsurumi was especially taken with the writings of a University of Wisconsin professor, Max Otto, who developed a philosophy of everyday life and believed that through language all problems could be solved; and Tsurumi deplored the fact that in his own country philosophers were narrowly specialized professionals who ignored human misery in their obsession with disinterested intellection, rather than devoted amateurs who might cultivate a holistic approach to human experience.[52]

Like most other things American, pragmatism was briefly popular in Japan after the war, not least as a means of discovering why America had won it. Tsurumi's book was written at the peak of fashion for American ideas, but beyond mere chance factors, the book reflected some genuine excitement. Pragmatism had lain in his way, but its open-minded emphasis on the testability of ideas in action appealed to his youthful non-conformist spirit. Marxists had been quick to equate pragmatism with imperialism and to scorn its intellectual pretensions; but Tsurumi, while sympathetic to some degree with Marxist social views, thought Marxists were too "mechanical" in their attitudes:

> Is it logical to look at the stage of production relations or production power and to require that history be explained in terms of inevitability?[53]

He regretted that the Japanese had tended to regard pragmatism as merely another "system," and he thought it incor-
rigible of them as of the Germans to court metaphysics and
find "thought" so pleasant that they separated it from other
human activities. James might, as his critics in Japan asserted,
have ignored economic factors in the human story, he may
have shown little interest in history at all; but reading James
had led Tsurumi to wonder about the role of accident, of
feeling, of psychology in the study of human behavior. Above
all, James had shown him that "the mind is not a closed box
but transcends the reach of the individual and communicates
with other minds."[54] He wanted other Japanese to feel the
excitement he felt over such ideas; and while he might wish
sometimes that pragmatism could acquire a more "tragic"
dimension and thus reach more deeply into Japanese life, he
continued to celebrate James' love of "exceptions," and in
later life he remained faithful to his early infatuation with the
classical pragmatist thinkers:

> I recognize that pragmatism has aspects that serve imperialism;
> but the pragmatism of Peirce, James and Mead cannot be dis-
> missed as a whole as the philosophy of imperialism.[55]

III

In the spring of 1946, Tsurumi joined a number of other
intellectuals to form a small study group calling itself the
Institute of the Science of Thought (*Shisō no Kagaku Kenkyūkai*). Instrumental in bringing the members together was his
older sister, Kazuko, who had studied at Vassar College while
he was at Middlesex School and who later received her Ph.D.
in sociology at Princeton. Kazuko had been repatriated with
Shunsuke on the *Gripsholm;* he owed a great deal to her
enterprise and energy at a time after the war when he was
nearly immobilized by illness and depression and knew virtually no one in Japan. In addition to the Tsurumis, original
members of the Science of Thought group included the econ-

omist Tsuru Shigeto, also repatriated on the *Gripsholm;* Maruyama Masao, the political scientist; two physicists, Taketani Mitsuo and Watanabe Satoshi; and the intellectual historian Takeda Kiyoko. The stated goal of the group was to produce research using empirical methods while maintaining a diversity of outlook and ideology. The group's journal, *Shisō no Kagaku,* which still endured in 1985, listed only two requirements for articles: they should be understandable, and their findings should be verifiable by "experience or logic."[56]

R. P. Dore has noted that few of the members of the Science of Thought group were social scientists in the sense of having had a rigorous theoretical training; yet while their writings were open to criticism as impressionistic, tendentious and lacking in theoretical sophistication, they stood for rationality and modern research methods. Their journal was devoted to

> promoting the outlook of Logical Empiricism in philosophy, fostering the development of an empirical scientific approach in the social sciences, and at the same time trying to counter the tendency to excessive academic specialization by promoting a broad comprehensive outlook on human problems as a whole.[57]

Group members were self-conscious intellectuals who felt a heavy responsibility to set new moral and ethical as well as political goals; moreover, they shared a sense of urgency and felt a crying need to promote foreign knowledge after the relative isolation of the previous decades. The magazine gave Tsurumi an outlet for his writing, and the group provided a sounding board for his ideas. Over the next 25 years he was to publish at least twenty articles in *Shisō no Kagaku,* and he took a leading part in many of the group's joint research activities.

By the end of 1948, with no record in Japanese secondary schools, Tsurumi had nevertheless secured a post as part-time lecturer in philosophy at Kyoto University. In a sense, he could perform for Japanese universities the same kind of role that had been played by foreigners under contract in Meiji times. After a year as a part-timer, in 1949 he was made an assistant professor and was at Kyōdai when the Occupation ended in 1952. Unknown to the general reading public, he had a small reputation as a writer on popular culture and pragmatism. He was more of an outsider than most other intellectuals: the journalist Ōya Sōichi labelled the Tsurumis a "classic American family" by virtue of their long and intense American experience.[58] Neither brother nor sister had been old enough to suffer the worst period of Japanese conformist pressure before the war, when so many others had been forced or chose to recant their progressive views. Yet like many other Japanese writers in the late 1940s and early 1950s, Shunsuke found in ultranationalism a treasure-trove of object lessons; like others, too, he dreamed of "the people" in protest and revolution. His hope that a completely new society might be produced in Japan did not die until the Korean War, perhaps not until 1960. While he was skeptical of Marxism as a system to explain history and thought the Marxists too "deductive" in their thinking, he avoided outright repudiation of Marxism as "liberation." Sensitive to both religious and artistic ideas—he thought enough of his youthful poetry to include some of it in his collected works—he still wanted, in the words of his biographer, to "unite Marxist goals with pragmatic means."[59]

Once the traumas of the immediate postwar period had been lived through, Tsurumi began to sift through the wartime and prewar record, seeking to assign responsibility for what had happened and to come to terms with his own guilt feelings. War responsibility became a major theme of intellectual discourse in the 1950s. His father's move to the right before the war had long puzzled him and made him suspicious of "liberals" who came touting modernization and democracy. If such people had caved in to the powers-that-be before 1945 they might do so again; and he began to wonder why nearly every so-called "progressive" had recanted during the war or before it. Why had so many on the left gone directly to emperor-centered "fascism"? Why were there so few Japanese counterparts to Western communists like Gide, Spender or Koestler, who had abandoned the faith and reverted to what Tsurumi took to be a truly liberal humanism? Why had the Japanese on

the repatriation ship lost the edge of their individual differences in a moment and exuded an aroma of cultural uniformity
that up until then had been concealed from view? Ever since
1944 Tsurumi had entertained an idea of writing about the
phenomenon of ideological recantation; his earliest writings on
this subject had been printed in the magazine *Me,* in that
year.[60] At some point in the early 1950s, after the book on
pragmatism had been finished, he decided to organize a research project that would utilize the resources of the Science
of Thought group in a full-scale examination of recantation
from before the war. To facilitate his own part in this project,
in 1954 he moved his base to Tokyo and took up a post in
philosophy at Tokyo Engineering University.

Recantation: A Cooperative Research Project (Kyōdō
Kenkyū: Tenkō) appeared in three large volumes between 1959
and 1962. It went through some thirteen printings, and a
revised edition was issued in 1978. Twenty-one authors, two of
them women, contributed signed articles; one author was
described as belonging to the prewar generation, seven to the
wartime generation, and thirteen to the postwar generation.
Tsurumi's contributions amounted to 175 pages in a total of
1300.[61]

Each volume was headed by a chapter (by Fujita Shōzō) on
the "objective situation" in each of three moments in modern
Japanese history: after the Manchurian invasion, just before
Pearl Harbor, and the Occupation. Volume I focused on prewar
recantation of Communists and other leftists and was centered
around the events of the early 1930s. Volume II dealt with
wartime collaborators, while Volume III covered postwar
adapters to the new democratic era. The main body of the
work consisted of biographical sketches and case studies based
on interviews and written sources, describing the careers and
attempting to uncover the motives for recantation of prominent
individuals with public reputations, grouped broadly according
to their ideological proclivities. The result was a kind of
encyclopedic guide to the positions taken by many of the best
known and some not so well known Japanese as the country
passed into and out of a posture of military aggressiveness

toward the rest of Asia and the democratic West in the years
between 1931 and 1952.

Tenkō was defined in an introductory chapter, written by
Tsurumi, as a "change of thought occurring because of force
exerted by the powers-that-be (*kenryoku*), especially the
state."[62] However, this definition was hardly adhered to very
rigorously; and while the authors sought, no doubt sincerely,
to avoid writing a mere exposé, one was tempted to use the
index (another example of Western influence) to look up people in whom one might be interested to learn how they had
behaved; the present author himself recalls how avidly some
of his Tokyo friends seized upon the gossip value of the work
when it first appeared.

No doubt the researchers were unsympathetic to those who
had recanted their beliefs, communist or otherwise. Yet they
were sensitive to the complexities of the whole subject, and
wished to avoid self-righteous moral judgements: Tsurumi
himself found a link between his earlier writings on pragmatism
and his effort to pursue a "pragmatic," relativistic approach
in dealing with the subject of recantation.[63] As a result, *Tenkō*
as a work of analysis lacked a clear-cut point of view. Aware
that it was writing what amounted to a work of mass exorcism
for the record of three decades of Japanese history, the Science of Thought group insisted that it had begun its work by
casting out the notion that only those who had not recanted
were "right." Yet while by neither clearly condoning nor
condemning others the group might avoid invidious judgments
or character assassination, it ran the risk of seeming a mere
bōkansha or "bystander," presenting a series of descriptive
vignettes of individual cases but ending with few conclusions
other than the obvious one: namely, that, in the Japanese case,
the alternatives to recantation had been scarce.

How the human subjects of the research were parcelled out
to contributors was not clear, but Tsurumi's portion included
some score of individuals, among them Konoe Fumimaro,
Ozaki Hotsumi, Shimizu Ikutarō, Ōya Sōichi, Ōkuma Nobuyuki and others—a variety of prominent people from different
callings and statuses, whom one suspects he chose because he

had an interest in them or perhaps felt some affinity for them; a few, at least, had had some relationship with his own family.

Two "cases" may give some idea of his subject matter. One of the more intriguing examples of recantation was a writer and Communist Party member, Haniya Yutaka, who progressed from Marx via Kantian metaphysics to "Oriental" thought while in prison—a not unfamiliar paradigm. Tsurumi's treatment of Haniya illustrates the combination of fact and rather impressionistic probing into personalities that was characteristic of much of the *Tenkō* book. Haniya's recantation occurred after he became convinced that a revolution was impossible for Japan in the early 1930s. Among his "influences" were Taoism, Hinduism, Buddhism, Jainism, Kierkegaard, Poe, Dostoyevsky, Rimbaud and Nietzsche. But the constraints of space prohibited Tsurumi from analyzing very many of these in an enlightening way, and the foreign reader, at least, was left with the uncomfortable feeling that the discussion was reducing itself to lists of names that might send some sort of tremor of recognition among some Japanese, but one could not be sure. In the end, one had to take on faith Tsurumi's statement that Haniya was modern Japan's most representative thinker.[64]

The "case" of Konoe Fumimaro, a better known figure, Tsurumi pursued as an example of what he called "failed false *tenkō*," or Konoe's attempt to conceal his own convictions that ended in self-deception and a move from private pretended recantation to ultimate leadership of the "fascist" Imperial Rule Assistance Association. Tsurumi's conclusions about Konoe did not add much to what was already known: he stressed Konoe's archaic connections with the imperial family and the shallow nature of his modernism. A man who, it was said, had been reading Oscar Wilde's *De Profundis* before taking poison to avoid trial as a war criminal, Konoe had recanted his earlier "liberal" professions out of too little sense of self *(kojinshugi no kashō)*. He had played with upper-class estheticism, Shirakaba-style; he had sensed that mystical *kokutai* was a dubious concept but he seemed never to have thought very deeply about it. He had wanted the League of

Nations to reject big-power imperialism and outlaw discrimination against yellow peoples yet he sanctioned the invasion of China by Japan. In the end, "there was another Konoe within Konoe," one keenly aware that his family had served the imperial house since the seventh century.[65]

The Science of Thought researchers concluded that few Japanese had recanted their beliefs out of any deeply held principles: most had been swept away, succumbing to shrewd or brutal inducements or to a kind of national intoxication with the slogans of the day. Yet some readers felt that there were deeper springs to the recantation phenomenon that were left only half-examined; the subject had been struck only a glancing blow. This, at least, could be concluded from the critical reception of the *Tenkō* volumes. The narrow definition of *tenkō* in terms of external pressures invited criticism. The poet and critic Yoshimoto Takaaki, in his own exploration of the subject, interpreted *tenkō* primarily as a personal strategem to rediscover a place in a community, to come in from the cold of superficial radical ideas and rejoin the warmth of the Japanese *kyōdōtai*. From a slightly different viewpoint, Maruyama Masao complained that the proposed definition of *tenkō* paid too little attention to subjective values: recantation might have religious dimensions that had little to do with force exerted by the state.[66]

Included in the revised edition of *Tenkō* were some critical essays on the work. Some writers saw it as too unscientific, a kind of "PTA of ideas." Others faulted the emphasis on individuals at the expense of organizations like the Communist Party with responsibility for protest against the emperor system and the military. Still others found too little stress on ethical principles: a "relativistic" approach had "bleached and flattened" the concept of recantation. The researchers were too dispassionate, not involved enough in the pains of those who had suffered torture or death at the hands of the special police. Others faulted the absence of stress on the simple concept of loyalty to the state, which had operated in many individual cases.[67]

Tsurumi himself by the late 1970s had come to realize that

recantation as a topic for analysis had lost much of its appeal
in the atmosphere of economic prosperity, the decline of
ideological confrontation within Japan and the diminution of
the state's charisma. Yet he also appeared aware that there
were depths in the subject still to be explored. He recounted
an anecdote concerning the meeting of the noted Christian
social worker Kagawa Toyohiko with Mahatma Gandhi during
the Second World War, when Gandhi allegedly told Kagawa to
return to Japan and go to jail for his beliefs. Kagawa returned
but was used by the military to broadcast to the West. When
asked about this afterward, Kagawa said that he had been
concerned not to do harm to those who had depended upon
him and believed in him. Tsurumi explained that this did not
mean that Kagawa was either inferior or superior to Gandhi; it
merely said something about Japanese views of Christianity
and ideological constancy. Tsurumi concluded that Gandhi's
form of non-violent resistance was regarded as a "heresy" by
Japanese Christians and that in order to understand the phenomenon of recantation fully Japanese intellectuals should
look at it from the outside, through the eyes of the "third
world."[68]

There can be no doubt that by the time of writing *Tenkō*
Tsurumi's disenchantment with American foreign policies had
grown very deep. When one of his "cases," Yoshida Mitsuru,
a survivor of the sinking of the battleship *Yamato*, turned up
in New York after the defeat, Yoshida discovered to his alarm
that Americans seemed to have no sense of guilt for the war
and were ready to kill again if another war came—which led
Tsurumi to reflect that Japanese who worked in the United
States for a few years were liable to lose their faith in Christian
civilization. Yet he showed equally little faith in Japan's own
new democratic institutions:

Wars in the late 20th century are fueled not so much by one
soldier killing another as by one bureaucrat or company man
killing many men with one memorandum. Most Japanese since
the war have been bureaucrats or company men, not soldiers.
But this doesn't guarantee that Japan has changed from milita-

rism to pacifism. Just as before the defeat soldiers were asked to give their highest loyalty to the commands of the state, so today the same question is asked of company men and bureaucrats.[69]

His anxiety about war and betrayal of democratic principles grew more intense after the publication of *Tenkō;* and in the atmosphere of sharpening political confrontation in the late 1950s, he lamented that no individual's ideas were reached in a completely reasoned way, but that all minds were subject to "shocks and vibrations," and the history of ideas was linked to "subjective experience."[70]

IV

Tsurumi's account of recantation had focused on intellectuals and others in the Japanese elite; ordinary citizens were not a subject of study. However, much of his time and energy in the 1950s was taken up with writing essays on aspects of popular culture: films, comic strips, *manzai, rakugo,* advertising—all came in for comment or content analysis, often by comparison with the media in America, which he used freely to diagnose the ills of both societies. In a small book published in 1958 entitled *What Can We Learn from American Thought? (Amerika Shisō kara Nani wo Manabu ka?),* his focus shifted from scholarly descriptions of 19th-century pragmatism to a disgruntled polemic against virtually the whole of contemporary American culture. It was the fashion in Japan in the 1950s and 1960s to pillory America as its Cold War policies alarmed more Japanese, but Tsurumi's attack was a particularly ironic reversal of his earlier position. Latter-day utopians such as Scott Nearing, or the Marxist economists, Paul Sweezy and Leo Huberman, were now compared unfavorably with Emerson and Thoreau. The misanthropic poet of the Monterey peninsula, Robinson Jeffers, was held up as a symbol of the blight on American culture as a whole. Tsurumi excoriated such scholars as the political scientist Harold Lasswell, whom he held responsible for the emergence of a new department of learning called "policy science," that, he thought, was at the beck and call of the nefarious state. However, at the same time, he noted that Japan had sung no dirges for its civilization that could convey the emotional depth of *Death of a Salesman* or *A Streetcar Named Desire;* and even as he lambasted American advertising and other facets of pop culture, he retained enough detachment to believe that the Cold War might one day end and Japan and the United States might again experience a closeness such as Haniya Yutaka had felt for Western ideas while serving time in Japanese prisons.[72]

By 1960 Tsurumi had solidified his reputation in the Japanese intellectual world. In a period when Marxist categories permeated intellectual discourse, like many others he remained sympathetic to the Marxist view of society in general but skeptical about the "formal logic" of the dialectic. In this period also he revealed a talent for synthesis of intellectual trends in a small compass. In 1956 he and Kuno Osamu published a text on *Modern Japanese Thought (Gendai Nihon no Shisō)*, to which Tsurumi contributed chapters on communist thought, Japanese pragmatism, existentialism, and the Shirakaba literary coterie.[73] In another short book entitled *Postwar Japanese Thought (Sengo Nihon no Shisō)*, written with Kuno and Fujita Shōzō,[74] he pursued his interest in pop culture with a chapter on the so-called "life composition movement" *(seikatsu tsuzurikata undō)*, through which some teachers were trying to get students to express themselves by keeping diaries recording their daily activities. Tsurumi was aware that such "movements" often had been fostered by leftist teachers; he was also aware that nurturing a critical spirit in children without a sense of striving or competition presented difficulties; yet he was intrigued with the "composition movement" because he saw it as an effort to build something out of Japanese particulars, something different from American-style democracy with its coloration of "rational competitiveness."[75] The urge to be free somehow of the flypaper of American influences ran through his writing and grew deeper as Japan, at least in his mind, became more and more dangerously enmeshed in American policies in Asia.

During the Security Treaty (*Ampo*) crisis in May–June 1960 Tsurumi achieved some notoriety as one of the leaders of a protest organization calling itself the "Voiceless Voices" ("Koe Naki Koe no Kai").[76] Prime Minister Kishi had allegedly asserted that the masses of voiceless Japanese supported the new treaty with the United States and that only the minority who were noisily demonstrating were against his government. The "Voiceless Voices" was meant to repudiate Kishi's statement, and it gained a brief fame among the various citizens' groups that sprang up during the summer of 1960.

Perhaps following the example of Takeuchi Yoshimi, Tsurumi resigned his post at Tokyo Engineering University in protest against the "forced adoption" of the treaty; however, unlike Takeuchi, he issued no proclamations, and in comparison with some other intellectuals of his circle he wrote little about the *Ampo* period. In 1975 he summed up his views on the protest movement:

> Our basic judgement was that war was bad, and we wanted to oppose it. Moreover, we feared America would embroil Japan in a war under its command. Those who forced through the Security Treaty were the same who had pushed the fifteen-year war [i.e., the Pacific War]. And we feared they were merely repeating their past political behavior. This was our simplistic judgement as political amateurs. In the sense that it preserved this simplistic judgement . . . the "Voiceless Voices" was a marvellous organization in the 1960s.[77]

Once the *Ampo* crisis had ended, Tsurumi wrote:

> Every time there is a large group shift of ideology in Japanese political history, there is an attempt to return to familiar vocabulary and to try to draw new wisdom from it. After the defeat of *Ampo* in 1960, we repeated such a situation.[78]

Mass protest was now shelved as the attention of the people shifted to economic objectives after 1960. Tsurumi in company with a number of other intellectuals turned rather self-consciously toward a search for roots. Though he cautioned against a useless attempt to resurrect the past entire, he repeated his conviction that more attention had to be paid to the values of the common people, and in the backlash of confrontation he was particularly attracted to the work of the ethnologist Yanagita Kunio, whose writings enjoyed a considerable vogue in the 1960s. After the heat of the protest movement, Tsurumi was attracted to images of a simpler time invoked in Yanagita's writings about village life and customs:

> To Yanagita, the idea of his own family was linked with thinking about the history of all his forebears. And the heart that wishes for the eternity of one's family is the heart that wishes for the prosperity of the country, composed as it is of village after village, all of them collections of families.[79]

Few such sentiments could be found in his earlier writings; but now he quoted approvingly the dictum of the poet Tanikawa Gan, that the language of the farmers was what held the Japanese people together,[80] and he called for a reinvigoration of the written language with idioms drawn from the vernacular. Yet most of the writers he quoted were still Westerners, and he seemed the perfect embodiment of what Katō Shūichi had in mind when he described Japanese culture as a hybrid of Western and indigenous elements.[81] The trouble was that while many Japanese could agree with this formulation with their minds, it left them feeling incompleted and dissatisfied; and even as he worried that the Japanese family might again be susceptible to manipulation by the state, Tsurumi saw deeply into the dilemma of "progressive" intellectuals like himself:

> Even without the clear violence of state power, progressive ideas that disregard the native tradition are over time changed by the force of surrounding customs. . . . When one's native soil comes up from the bottom of one's memory, progressive ideas can seem unbearable and be easily abandoned.[82]

After all the "struggles" and protest demonstrations of the fifteen years after the war, he sounded a note of deep frustra-

tion, not just with what America had become since his days at
Middlesex School but with all of European and Russian civilization as well:

> The principle of thinking of people as one, as a universal unity,
> whether they are connected with one by blood or not, is to be
> sought. But belief in this principle cannot appeal to the contem-
> porary Japanese masses as much as it did to youth in Meiji and
> Taishō times. Latter-day youth have seen the colonial record of
> Western civilization, the oppression and slaughter of the Jews,
> the dropping of the atomic bomb, and the purges in communist
> countries. Knowing as we do that universalism has its own
> peculiar cruelty, we cannot think it is good to cast aside our own
> family gods and attach ourselves to a god of universal princi-
> ples.[83]

He praised what he called Japan's "anthological" culture, a
culture highly selective in its elements, whose view of each
single concrete human life was very different, he thought, from
Western humanism's view of mankind. Japanese had only a
vague idea of the utter destruction of the flesh. Men could
always change their ideas; Christians or communists could
apostatize, just as many former militarists had done under the
Occupation. Perhaps, after all, *tenkō* was intrinsic to the
Japanese spirit; and although this changeableness might mean
a betrayal of idealism in the abstract, was there not a certain
generosity about it that was peculiarly Japanese?[84] Yet his
ambivalence toward the West and Japan's need for it remained
strong:

> Nobody in Japanese mythology was a special god, anybody
> could be thought a god; from the Japanese religious spirit in
> which nature and animals stood equal to man and could be
> approached with intimacy came a universal principle. . . . But at
> present there is no way but to look squarely at the lack of a
> concept of a universal principle in Japanese culture, and to fill
> the gap with borrowed universal principles. Borrowed things will
> remain in Japanese thought for a long time to come.[85]

In November 1960, shortly after his marriage, Tsurumi suffered another bout of mental depression and withdrew from society for nearly a year. In late 1961 he took a position at Dōshisha University in Kyoto, where he remained until the student disturbances of 1968–69, when he finally gave up teaching entirely. Tokyo had become more and more unliveable to him, and he remained in Kyoto, where he yearned for Thoreau's simple life.[86] More convinced than ever that direct experience and action were the only valid guides to conduct, he quoted George Orwell and Aldous Huxley; the latter's *The Doors of Perception* seems to have interested him in the psychedelic drug phenomenon. In the early 1960s, as a small gesture expressive of his frustrations and feelings of guilt, he and two of his friends decided to have their heads shaved *in seriatim* each August 15 to mark the defeat in 1945. In 1970 he was still brooding over his failure to do anything against the war.[87] Above all he wished for some organic connection with the native Japanese world even as he yearned for more contact with the world outside Japan:

> I want to separate myself from the traces in my thought that led me to be cornered into silent cooperation with the Japanese state during the war. I want to reintegrate the ideas that became my excuse for such a course—a certain amount of liberalism and pragmatism, and an insufficiency of knowledge about class consciousness and the structure of imperialism: a weakness in the springs that tied my ideas to action. . . . I want to analyze these ideas and think about the form of their rebirth. . . . I want to go back to my birth and live in a different way. Individual shame over the past is now a prime moving force [in me]. . . . We must not only go back to the local nature of Japan, we must also find connections with things international.[88]

Again and again he battled with his guilt about the war:

> I could do nothing against the war during it. I continued to write against it in my diary. I spoke to people I could trust. But I could do no more than that. I thought I wanted to, but I didn't lift a finger. . . . Rather than feeling despair toward the war I felt it toward myself.[89]

And these guilt feelings led him to bring his whole intellectual enterprise, including his work on recantation, into question:

> I looked at Japan during the war as material to work on, using the method of logical positivism. . . . The material was part of the situation but the method was outside it, and I would look in from outside. I now think this way of looking at the method was an illusion, but it took time during and after the war for me to know this. It was obvious, but I was long in noticing it. Logical positivism's scientific viewpoint was itself a [self-conscious] choice.[90]

V

In 1965, as American involvement in the Vietnam War grew in scope and intensity, some Japanese intellectuals sought to mobilize opposition to the war and to Japan's cooperation with American policies. One of them, Professor Takabatake Michitoshi, of Rikkyō University, a former member of the "Voiceless Voices," suggested to Tsurumi that demonstrations be mounted against the American bombings of North Vietnam and the use of staging bases in Okinawa and elsewhere in Japan. Tsurumi contacted Oda Makoto, well known for his writings about his travels in the West, and Oda, Takabatake and Tsurumi, along with some others, became leaders of a new protest organization to be known as *Beheiren (Betonamu ni Heiwa wo! Shimin Bunka Dantai Remmei),* or the League for Peace in Vietnam.[91] Most of the people who participated in *Beheiren* came from a generation younger than Tsurumi's; they sought to identify not just with an intellectual elite but with the "common man" of the "third world." They felt little or no guilt for World War II and were unaware that they suffered from any problem of "teleological insight." More women joined *Beheiren,* though women were still in a minority; and the spirit or "lifestyle" of its members was closer to the Japanese version of the "new left" than to the *Ampo* generation.

As *Beheiren* became involved in seeking to persuade American military personnel to desert from their units, Tsurumi's views about the United States continued to change. By 1967 he was imagining how he might rewrite his 1950 book on American philosophy to reflect his new concerns:

> If I wrote that book now I would truly want to rewrite it. What would American philosophy be, how would it operate from the standpoint of blacks? Or I would like to treat it from the viewpoint of Cubans. . . . The history of Japanese thought would be the same. . . . How does Japan look from the viewpoint of Koreans in Japan?[92]

At the same time his faith in parliamentary institutions had weakened: "Saying that the majority party is good and that we must necessarily follow it in every respect merely means that we are beaten."[93] The Vietnam War reactivated his long-standing fear of nuclear destruction and deepened his hatred of his country's leaders, long seen as rogues and turncoats: "Those who formerly made war became Prime Ministers. . . ."[94] Meanwhile he busied himself collecting money for advertisements in American newspapers opposing the war, helped arrange for a boat in which to sail around an American aircraft carrier to call on sailors to desert, and flew kites around the periphery of Iwakuni air base in a symbolic gesture against the bombing of Vietnam. *Beheiren,* as he saw it, was a step toward "participatory democracy" of a kind Thoreau would have approved. Like some other protestors he was not slow to set his own definition of the laws above that of the civil authorities of the time:

> I felt that acts that the authorities of the day might classify as a crime might from another social-ethical point of view, by becoming acts of non-surrender, be a source of independent strength.[95]

In 1971 Tsurumi took another book-length look at his American experience in the 1930s, this time with a focus on a rather different cast of characters. He wrote at length of the career of F. O. Matthiessen, the noted Harvard professor of English and critic of American literature, who had been a Christian socialist and head of the Harvard Teachers Union when Tsurumi was a student there. Praising Matthiessen's acceptance of the responsibility of the critic to engage with social issues, Tsurumi lamented his 1950 suicide.[96] About such people as Matthiessen Tsurumi had written nothing in his earlier accounts of America; Matthiessen's career was more "relevant" now, when America's actions in the world seemed to him bleak and forbidding. Now he attacked America as a racist society, not mentioning the accomplishments of the Johnson administration in the sphere of civil rights. With his revised insight he thought it strange for Japanese to identify, as he had once, with whites; and he suddenly realized that he had never met a native American.[97] Even Matthiessen's *American Renaissance* had had nothing much to say about Indians.

In this installment of Tsurumi's running dispute with the United States, the "new left," not William James or George Herbert Mead, took center-stage; yet he professed astonishment at how closely American anti-war activists followed in the steps of William James in equating thought with action![98] Now he was powerfully attracted to the new lifestyles that sought, among other things, a return to more closeness with nature, a "greening" of America, if not Japan. Emerson had written that no man was without the possibility of greatness.[99] Now Tsurumi appeared to believe that to achieve his true stature, man needed to embrace the "small is beautiful" ideal. He wrote enthusiastically of the poet Gary Snyder and the vogue of Zen Buddhism in America, hailed the arrival of a new sense of community among the younger generation there, and wanted to resuscitate the "power of savage man" via poetry to get back into the "play of the universe." Approving of the "life of the tribe," he thought the noble savage ideal needed reviving:

> Without entrusting ourselves to outside powers; preserving the notion that man's life as it is is worth trusting; opposing a system of national scale; such thinking is taken to be dangerous for

modern civilization. . . . But in the midst of heavily armed modern states, tribes are growing up, that comprise streams of lower-strata culture from primitive times.[100]

However perverse and ill-judged his activities in *Beheiren* might have appeared to the powers-that-be, Tsurumi was deeply moved by a second chance to protest in the late 1960s and early 1970s, when he might take some action, however ineffectual, as he had not during the Pacific war. And this time, he would try to take blacks, Indians, even Inuit, into account. When Howard Zinn and Ralph Featherstone went to tour Japan as representatives of the Student Non-Violent Coordinating Committee (SNCC), Tsurumi served as their interpreter; he could not accompany them to Okinawa, where *Beheiren* was banned, but Featherstone put up at Tsurumi's house in Kyoto, and he wrote of Featherstone's later activities until the latter's death in 1970. Reading Eldridge Cleaver's *Soul on Ice,* Tsurumi thought he understood better his own period of study in the United States.[101] Now he professed to believe that the "pragmatism" of SNCC was more "pragmatic" than John Dewey's progressive education schemes had been; yet he still stood up for the classical pragmatists: "the philosophy of Peirce and Mead cannot be thrown out simply as the philosophy of imperialism."[102]

The greater problem was how to use the freedom and exhilaration he obviously derived from the protest movement to arrive at some more lasting Japanese design for living or purpose for the culture that would be rooted in non-authoritarian values but would not merely mimic foreign ideas or repeat outworn Japanese ones. For this voyage Tsurumi had many fellow-travellers but few landmarks. Characteristically, in reflecting on the Vietnam era he fell back on a critique of the deficiencies in human communication among the Japanese. He had spent decades criticizing the parochial obscurantism of Japanese academics and trying to spread knowledge of how people communicated with one another in the West. How many Japanese, he asked, had been able to move people in the outside world through their writing or speaking? Almost none,

he thought. When two Japanese strangers of different ages
could not even communicate meaningfully with each other in
the train, how could Japan produce a Descartes, a Bacon, or a
Leibnitz? He longed mightily for a greater openness, a more
"playful spirit" *(asobi no seishin)* in the culture as a whole as
well as in the language of philosophical expression, a more
truly liberal and tolerant cosmopolitanism that would somehow
be based on firm local roots as well as on supranational
experience.[103] Alas, men and women with such qualities were
in short supply anywhere.

Even such a person as Yanagi Muneyoshi (Sōetsu), the
esthetician and founder of the folk art *(mingei)* movement in
Japan, whose biography Tsurumi wrote in the 1970s and whom
he greatly admired, did not quite measure up to this ideal
standard. True, Yanagi had been deeply influenced by William
Blake, had read Blake's poetry as a young man and been fired
by his revolutionary fervor. True again, Yanagi had shown a
profound interest in Korean art, at a time when few if any
other Japanese had done so. Yanagi had gone on to make a
cult of "beauty in usefulness" and to celebrate the "unknown
craftsman." Yet for all his passion for Korean art, there
remained the nagging feeling that the Korean critic might be
right who claimed that Yanagi knew little about the "real lives"
of those Korean "masses" who made the beautiful objects he
so admired. To this critic, Yanagi had been a victim of the
colonialist presumptions of his period; without humor about
Korea or its art, he saw folk art only in terms of formal objects,
not the lives of their makers. Ignoring the "social context"
and fixing upon art for its own sake, his intuitions of artistic
value were somehow suspect. And Tsurumi was left with the
uncomfortable suspicion that little comfort was to be had in
contemplating Japan's spiritual or artistic communion with the
"third world."[104]

VI

Tsurumi Shunsuke's grandfather, Gotō Shimpei, physician and
busy bureaucrat, had stood for the embrace of Western science

and technology to build a modern state. Tsurumi's father, Yūsuke, "courtly and charming" to at least one American, had spent years explaining to other Americans the interests of the state that Gotō had helped to build. After the Pacific war, amid the ruins of Gotō's and Yūsuke's endeavors, Shunsuke displayed an ambivalence toward both state and society that was born of his upbringing as well as Japan's total defeat, a rebelliousness foreign to either Gotō's or Yūsuke's world. Gotō had shared the limelight with the Meiji "greats"; Yūsuke fit with apparent ease into parliamentary politics before and after 1945. But Shunsuke, whose knowledge of Western life and history was deeper than either of the other two, turned intellectual gadfly, nursing his hurts inwardly by writing and outwardly living out his beliefs in demonstrations. Few called him either courtly or charming. What, one wonders, would Gotō have thought of his "pragmatic" grandson?

It was easy to be impatient with Tsurumi, to low-rate his idealism, to charge that his kite-flying at Iwakuni, like *Beheiren*'s incitements to American servicemen and other such activities, were mere sterile provocations meant to prove the mettle of his nationalism, gestures that put him at little personal risk and that, though they may have got the adrenalin flowing, hardly changed the "objective situation" very much. Yet his behavior might have been predicted. He had been taught at prep school and college in Massachusetts to seek the meaning of experience by putting ideas to the test of action. His "role models" came out of a New England village rather than from Japanese neo-Confucian teachers. He was a doubter even before he went to Middlesex School, but American ideas and ideals supported his long series of symbolic gestures, whether made silently against the Pacific war, or more publicly against the new Security Treaty, or most spectacularly in *Beheiren*, whatever the efficacy or the moral equivocation of those gestures. If Gotō took the West's scientific and technological results as a Good, and Yūsuke adapted to the West's institutional surface, Shunsuke reached some distance farther toward its psychological and ethical depths. His disillusionment, when it came, was therefore especially powerful.

Tsurumi Shunsuke's most significant contribution to his time was not made in the realm of theory; there are few alluring hypotheses or *ketsuron* in his writings. However, he applied his powers of observation and his training in the testing of data to a wide range of Japanese cultural forms after 1945, and he left a readable description of that world of mass communication and popular entertainment, or what he liked to call "marginal" art. As late as 1984 he was still publishing essays on newspaper comics, films, popular songs and the literature of the lending libraries,[105] as well as prize-winning essays in the "high" intellectual history of the period.[106] His content analyses of cartoon characters like "Sazae-san" and his sketches of the historical background and critical slant of genres like *manzai* and *rakugo* were often more interesting, at least to the foreign reader, than his more solemn explorations of the nuances of ideological shift and reversal in the *Tenkō* volumes. For the subject matter of the neighborhood theatres, the *yose,* was perennially alive, while recantation seemed a dead issue in the 1980s.

In his preoccupation with "the people" Tsurumi was of course representative of his whole generation; most intellectuals who came to maturity after the war were in their different ways obsessed with the regeneration of their society, and many turned to mass culture to find what Japanese "essence" they might identify as vital to the future of their country. Most were cultural nationalists before they were followers of any foreign ideology. Tsurumi was attracted to popular genres in part because he knew that through them the establishment could be criticized; but on a deeper level it was the tension between indigenous and imported cultural influences that fascinated him and concentrated his mind. In his most ambitious writings, including his writings on recantation, he showed that he was conscious of the difficulty of ever confronting this tension and fully resolving it, of sorting out for good what could be called "Japanese." But the effort had to be made again and again. And was Tsurumi's generation to be the last to have to deal with such an identity crisis?

In a 1960 article on the career of Nitobe Inazō, who had been a friend of Tsurumi's father and like him a propagandist for Japan's cause before 1941, Tsurumi discussed Nitobe's role as a self-styled "bridge" between East and West, his blend of Buddhist, Christian and Shinto-based beliefs, his so-called "situational ethics." Nitobe had been a "rational eclectic," a middle-level bureaucrat who had made a career of recommending conservative alternatives that had succeeded in the West to his superiors in government. He had placed more emphasis on will and virtue than on wisdom or learning; his emphasis on self-cultivation was matched or overshadowed by his loyalty to the imperial institution and the "polity" *(kokutai)*. Yet to Nitobe, *kokutai* had not meant an irrational myth or a mystical shibboleth, but rather something akin to Burke's conservative vision of government.[107] Nor was the emperor to Nitobe superhuman, but merely a kind of conservator of the memories of the people, an expression, as Tsurumi put it elsewhere, of the "religious yearning of Japanese culture for independence."[108] Nitobe had used late Meiji logic to try to explain away Shōwa facts of international life; in the last analysis, the West had not been taken in.[109] But even though Nitobe's "eclecticism" had done nothing to stop the slide to war, Tsurumi argued that emperor and *kokutai* had in the postwar period come to resemble Nitobe's conception of them; and he found something sympathetic in Nitobe's ideas without wishing to endorse their past political implications.

In Tsurumi one was left with an impression of a dilemma of tradition and modernity unreconciled. It was the dilemma of Japanese culture as a whole raised to a level of acute self-consciousness in an iconoclastic mind. Yet however provoking or contradictory his career might have been, he was a searcher who was unafraid to grow and change. It may be wondered how many other Japanese intellectuals at a late stage of their careers would have enshrined a whole new cast of characters in their pantheon of American heroes. How many would have kept on straining for as long as Tsurumi did for a redefinition of Japanese cultural distinctiveness that would incorporate

influences from the lives and writings of men as dissimilar as
Ralph Waldo Emerson, Yanagita Kunio, Gary Snyder and
Nitobe Inazō?

1985

Conclusion

The case studies in this book comprise four readings of the meaning of being Japanese that were part of the more general soul-searching after defeat in World War II. The essays were conceived and written as self-contained units, each with its own conclusion; therefore, no lengthy conclusion is needed to the whole.

The reader may nevertheless have been struck by the intensity of the concern with the meaning of Japanese nationality in these writers' lives and writings. Defining Japaneseness absorbed them in varying degrees over long careers; and while their discourse sometimes expressed a very human and universal quest for identity, from first to last it was bound by the constraints of the nationality it sought to redefine. E. M. Forster once wrote that "One may sympathize instinctively with those who talk of race and nationality, but civilization, which they often forget, is greater than these."* None of these four writers need be accused of forgetting civilization; yet even for those, like Etō and Tsurumi, with the greatest experience of the West, or Takeuchi, who spent his whole life studying China, the terms of *Japanese* nationality set the limit of their emotional outreach to others. Concerned always lest they be

---

*Quoting the Maharajah of Dewas, in *The Hill of Devi,* New York, Harcourt, Brace, 1953, p. 68.

153

less or other than Japanese, whatever that was to mean, these four writers, like most of their peers, wrote less often of themselves as simply men, located in the general human predicament, than as bearers of a special and peculiar Japanese identity. That identity had been the subject of repeated definition by writers and thinkers ever since the 19th century and before, as Japanese sought to keep their balance and succeed in the modern world. It was brought perilously low by defeat, and afterward, when catching up to the West seemed finally to have lost its point, it was left to the postwar generation to find new ways of fixing Japanese identity. This search for new approaches animated the writings of these four intellectuals.

For those like these four with the luxury of time for reflection and the duty of intellectual production, various paths presented themselves for the fulfillment of their self-assigned search. Takeuchi Yoshimi, extrapolating from Lu Xun's satires of traditional Chinese personality, thought he saw in Mao's China a flowering of self-respect, something he found weak or missing in modern Japanese life and therefore worth emulating. Tsurumi Shunsuke and Etō Jun, both deeply marked by their Western experience and thoroughly elitist in their recoil from the misshapenness of the Japanese world around them, took different routes away from the present and toward a more satisfactory world; the former found some release in the study of popular culture and in symbolic gestures of rebellion against the established order, while the latter drifted towards conservative nostalgia for conventional imperial "greatness." Yoshimoto Takaaki spent much of his energy excoriating the hypocrisy of others and proposing a stirring if not very clear idea of "the people" and their "independence" as the way out of what he saw as Japan's existential dilemma.

All these strategies were moral enough, serious, even solemn and imperfect solutions to identity problems that were unlikely ever to yield perfect solutions. That they even saw problems and sought solutions set them apart from most of their Japanese fellows and was what made them "intellectuals." Of the four, Tsurumi's "pragmatic" approach to the themes in his writings gave them a certain dispassionate clarity, while the other three veered toward passionate but unrealistic ideals. But being intellectuals, and being Japanese, they went on writing copiously, knowing that what they wrote would quickly be published, prospering as their society prospered, talking to one another, or past one another, in a language that almost none of their fellow intellectuals in other lands could understand, and that nearly nobody took the trouble to translate. All the more reason, then, to explore their thoughts, even though there might be few "great" ones among them. For while it was impossible to measure their influence, they assuredly influenced in ways beyond measure the many readers of their books and articles.

The quest for new cultural meaning had before it the fact of defeat at the hands of Western power that was anything but abstract, but touched every life. Etō may have had a point when he compared Japan in August 1945 with the American South just 80 years earlier. His feelings on returning to the wasteland of his old Ōkubo neighborhood must somehow, he thought, resemble the feelings of Confederate soldiers walking home from northern battlefields. Little wonder that intellectual discourse in the decades following the war was marked by sentiments of fear, guilt and recrimination, or that the West was regarded with suspicion as well as admiration. It had always been so; but now nuclear devastation merely strengthened Japan's conviction, already extreme, of its separateness from the balance of humanity. With a monopoly of such experience in their possession, and a sense of their helplessness to prevent the encroaching Cold War, how was openness of spirit to be expected, especially from intellectuals? How could they avoid a deep ambivalence toward the West from whence had come the gains of modernity as well as annihilation? Yoshimoto's flirtations with Christianity and Marxism, like Etō's distaste for American-style marriage or Tsurumi's refusal to work for the Occupation, all pointed to that ambivalence, which cut to the heart of modern Japanese self-consciousness.

Meanwhile, in the final reckoning, who in the West was listening? There, as before, Japan meant mainly merchandise—once matches that would not strike, now "high tech" that worked—or it meant the decorative arts. A few novelists, a few film makers, perhaps, but not philosophers, and not "intellectuals." Yet the pursuit of an understanding of themselves and their society by these four men, like other contemporary writers and thinkers, mirrored their country's predicament as part of the "post-modern" world yet ineffably uncomfortable within it. Until Japan's peculiar cultural situation was better understood, until the foreign and the native elements in the culture, the riches as well as the meagernesses that George Sansom long ago noted, were better integrated in the minds of Japan's intellectual leaders, the true and full meaning of Japaneseness would continue to elude a clearly expressed formulation by foreigners and Japanese alike.

Notes

CHAPTER 1

1. Interview with Etō Jun, Karuizawa, August 5, 1981.
2. Etō Jun, *Ichizoku Saikai,* Tokyo, Kōdansha Bunko, 1976, p. 138. First published 1973.
3. *Ibid.,* pp. 120–121.
4. *Ibid.,* p. 29.
5. *Ibid.,* p. 41.
6. *Ibid.,* p. 74.
7. Etō Jun, *Bungaku to Watakushi, Sengo to Watakushi,* Tokyo, Shinchō Bunko, 1974, p. 170.
8. His stepmother's father appears to have been a Christian who undertook to teach him English. *Ibid.,* p. 172.
9. *Ichizoku Saikai,* p. 328.
10. Etō Jun, *Natsume Sōseki,* Tokyo, Tokyo Life Co., 1956. All references are to the 1971 Kōdansha Bunko paperback edition.
11. *Ibid.,* pp. 28–29, 84.
12. *Ibid.,* pp. 69–70.
13. *Ibid.,* p. 26.
14. Jean-Paul Sartre, *Baudelaire,* New York, New Directions, 1950, p. 139. Etō read Sartre at this stage of his career and was especially impressed by this essay.
15. Etō Jun, "Nihon Bungaku to 'Watakushi'," *Shinchō,* March 1965, p. 190. Cf. also Etō Jun, "Natsume Sōseki, A Japanese Intellectual," *The American Scholar,* XXXIV, 1965, pp. 603–619.
16. *Ibid.,* p. 195.

17. *Bungaku to Watakushi, Sengo to Watakushi*, p. 146.

18. Quoted in Nihon Bungaku Kenkyū Shiryō Kankōkai, eds., *Nihon Bungaku Kenkyū Shiryō Sōsho: Yoshimoto Takaaki, Etō Jun*, Tokyo, Yuseidō, 1980, p. 166.

19. *Ibid.*

20. *Natsume Sōseki*, pp. 28–29.

21. Etō Jun, *Hyōgen toshite no Seiji*, Tokyo, Bungei Shunjū, 1969, pp. 447, 468.

22. *Ibid.*, p. 434.

23. Etō Jun, *Sakka wa kōdō suru*, Tokyo, Kadokawa Shoten, 1969, pp. 13, 33–36. First published in 1959.

24. *Ibid.*, p. 61. Italics in text.

25. *Ibid.*, p. 121.

26. *Ibid.*, p. 102.

27. *Ibid.*, p. 110.

28. *Ibid.*, pp. 126–127.

29. Thus he applauded such "progressives" as Noma Hiroshi for being a "participant" in the disorderly postwar scene, thought Haniya Yutaka had asked "existential questions," and praised Takeda Taijun for his "dynamic imagination." *Ibid.*, p. 172, ff.

30. Etō Jun, *Kobayashi Hideo*, Tokyo, Kōdansha Bunko, 1973, p. 33. First published in 1961.

31. *Ibid.*, pp. 129–130.

32. *Ibid.*, p. 269. Cf. also Edward G. Seidensticker, "Kobayashi Hideo," in Donald Shively, ed., *Tradition and Modernization in Japanese Culture*, Princeton, NJ, Princeton University Press, 1971.

33. *Ibid.*, pp. 269–270.

34. *Ibid.*, p. 257. Kobayashi had been a participant in the famous 1942 symposium on "Overcoming the Modern." Cf. *Kindai no Chōkoku*, Tokyo, Fūzambō, 1979.

35. Interview with Ōkubo Takaki, Tokyo, July 18, 1981.

36. *Kobayashi Hideo*, pp. 373–374, quoting Kobayashi.

37. For example, cf. Yamada Munemutsu, *Kiken-na Shisōka*, Tokyo, Kōbunsha, 1965, p. 127.

38. Etō Jun, *Hizuke no aru Bunshō*, Tokyo, Chikuma Shobō, 1960, p. 12.

39. *Ibid.*, p. 18.

40. *Ibid.*, p. 38.

41. Etō Jun, "The Bankruptcy of our Idealistic Intellectuals," *Journal of Social and Political Ideas in Japan*, II, 1, April 1964, p. 102. Text in English. For Japanese text, cf. *Bungei Shunjū*, November 1960, pp. 98–106.

42. *Ibid.*, pp. 102–105.
43. *Ibid.*, p. 106.
44. *Hizuke no aru Bunshō*, p. 47.
45. *Ibid.*, p. 55.
46. *Ibid.*, p. 117.
47. *Ibid.*, p. 189.
48. *Ibid.*, pp. 195–197.
49. Etō Jun, *Amerika to Watakushi*, Tokyo, Kōdansha Bunko, 1972, pp. 19–26. First published in 1965.
50. *Ibid.*, p. 48.
51. *Ibid.*, p. 82.
52. *Ibid.*, pp. 89–90.
53. *Ibid.*, p. 90.
54. *Ibid.*, p. 35.
55. *Ibid.*, p. 68.
56. *Ibid.*, p. 88.
57. *Ibid.*, pp. 73–74.
58. *Ibid.*, p. 102.
59. *Ibid.*, p. 190.
60. *Ibid.*, p. 136.
61. *Ibid.*
62. *Ibid.*, p. 152.
63. *Ibid.*, pp. 241–242.
64. *Ibid.*, p. 269.
65. *Ibid.*, p. 156.
66. *Ibid.*, p. 269.
67. *Ibid.*, p. 257.
68. *Ibid.*, pp. 270–273.
69. *Ibid.*, p. 264.
70. Etō Jun, "Old America and New Japan," *Journal of Social and Political Ideas in Japan,* III, 2, August 1965, p. 72.
71. Etō Jun, *Seijuku to Sōshitsu*, Tokyo, Kōdansha, 1978, p. 163. First published in 1967.
72. *Ibid.*, p. 59.
73. *Ibid.*, p. 75.
74. *Ibid.*, pp. 90–91.
75. *Ibid.*, p. 221.
76. *Ibid.*, p. 244.
77. *Bungaku to Watakushi, Sengo to Watakushi*, pp. 104, 110.
78. *Ibid.*, p. 191.
79. *Ibid.*, pp. 195–196.

80. Etō Jun, personal communication, December 29, 1981.

81. *Bungaku to Watakushi, Sengo to Watakushi*, p. 297.

82. Etō Jun, *Sōseki to Sono Jidai*, Tokyo, Shinchōsha, 1970, II, p. 93.

83. *Amerika to Watakushi*, p. 40.

84. *Bungaku to Watakushi, Sengo to Watakushi*, p. 62.

85. Etō Jun, *Kaishū Yoha*, Tokyo, Bungei Shunjū, 1974.

86. Etō Jun, *Umi wa Yomigaeru*, Tokyo, Bungei Shunjū, 1976, et. seq. Interview with Irokawa Daikichi, Tokyo, July 29, 1981.

87. *Kaishū Yoha*, pp. 330–331.

88. Japanese text in Etō Jun, "Shisha to no Kizuna," *Shinchō*, February 1980, p. 238. For English text, cf. footnote 89, below.

89. Etō Jun, "An Aspect of the Allied Occupation of Japan: The Censorship Operation and Postwar Japanese Literature," Washington, D.C., The Wilson Center, June 18, 1980, pp. 9–10. Typescript in English. Quoted by permission of the author.

90. "Shisha to no Kizuna," *Shinchō*, February 1980, p. 239.

91. Etō Jun, "Senryōgun no Ken'etsu to Sengo Nihon," *Shokun!*, February 1982, pp. 105–106.

92. Etō Jun, *1946 Kempō: Sono Kōsoku*, Tokyo, Bungei Shunjū, 1980, pp. 20–21.

93. Satō Seizaburō, "Kempō Rongi e no Gimon," *Koe*, April 1981, pp. 120–130. English-language version in *Japan Echo*, VIII, 2, 1981, pp. 94–103. Passage cited from English version, pp. 98–99.

94. *Ibid.*, pp. 99, 103.

95. *1946 Kempō: Sono Kōsoku*, p. 99.

96. *Ibid.*, pp. 93–94.

97. Etō Jun, *Hihyōka no Kimama-no Sampo*, Tokyo, Shinchōsha, 1973, p. 61.

98. *Ibid.*, p. 119.

99. Etō Jun, "An Aspect of the Allied Occupation of Japan," p. 16. Typescript in English. Quoted by permission.

100. Interview with Ōkubo Takaki, Tokyo, July 1981.

101. Quoted in Kikuta Hitoshi, *Etō Jun Ron*, Tokyo, Tōkisha, 1979, p. 87.

102. *Ibid.*, p. 118.

103. On this last point, cf. "Etō Jun vs. Irokawa Daikichi," *Asahi Jaanaru*, May 8, 1981, p. 19.

CHAPTER 2

1. Takeuchi Yoshimi, *Fufukujū no Isan*, Tokyo, Chikuma Shobō, 1961, pp. 106–107.

2. *Ibid.*, p. 177.

3. Noriko Kamachi, "Historical Consciousness and Identity: The Debate of China Specialists over American Research Funds," *Journal of Asian Studies*, XXXIV, 4, April 1975, pp. 990–991.

4. *Ibid.*, quoting Imahori Seiji, in turn quoting Kaizuka Shigeki.

5. *Ibid.*, pp. 991, 993.

6. Interview with Takeuchi Teruko, Tokyo, July 9, 1979.

7. Takeuchi Yoshimi, *Nihon to Chūgoku no Aida*, Tokyo, Bungei Shunjū, 1973, pp. 438–441; *Rojin*, Tokyo, Miraisha, 1961, p. 202.

8. Interview with Takeuchi Teruko, Tokyo, July 9, 1979.

9. Takeuchi, *Nihon to Chūgoku no Aida*, pp. 446–454; Matsumoto Ken'ichi, *Takeuchi Yoshimi Ron*, Tokyo, Dai San Bummeisha, 1975, p. 88.

10. Honda Shūgo, *Sengo Bungakushi*, Tokyo, Shinchōsha, 1966, pp. 490–491; Matsumoto, *op. cit.*, p. 32.

11. Interview with Hashikawa Bunzō, New York, November 14, 1978.

12. *Nihon to Chūgoku no Aida*, p. 447.

13. Itakura Shōhei, "Takeuchi Yoshimi to Takeda Taijun," *Asahi Jaanaru*, January 24, 1972, p. 37.

14. Quoted in Honda, *op. cit.*, p. 491.

15. *Nihon to Chūgoku no Aida*, p. 182.

16. Takeuchi Yoshimi, *Jōkyōteki (Taidanshū)*, Tokyo, Gōdō Shuppan Sha, 1970, p. 191. His biographer states that he was dissatisfied with Marxist explanations, complaining that in Marxism "man is absent." Cf. Matsumoto, *op. cit.*, p. 36.

17. *Nihon to Chūgoku no Aida*, p. 333.

18. *Ibid.*, p. 335.

19. *Takeuchi Yoshimi Hyōronshū*, Tokyo, Chikuma Shobō, 1966 (hereafter cited as *TYHS*), III, pp. 323–325.

20. *Ibid.*, pp. 227–232.

21. *Nihon to Chūgoku no Aida*, p. 224.

22. Takeuchi Yoshimi, *Hōhō toshite no Ajia*, Tokyo, Sokisha, 1978, pp. 42, ff.

23. *Nihon to Chūgoku no Aida*, pp. 532–533.

24. *Ibid.*, p. 534.

25. *Ibid.*, p. 273.

26. *Ibid.*, p. 534.

27. *TYHS*, I, pp. 47–49.

28. *Nihon to Chūgoku no Aida*, p. 533.

29. Takeuchi Yoshimi, *Rojin*, Tokyo, Miraisha, 1961, p. 200.

30. Lu Xun, *Wild Grass*, Beijing, Foreign Languages Press, 1974, p. 32.

31. *TYHS*, I, p. 12 (written in June 1948).

32. Katō Shūichi, *Katō Shūichi Chosakushū*, Tokyo, Heibonsha, 1979, VII, pp. 272, ff.

33. Quoted in *ibid.*, p. 270.

34. *TYHS*, III, p. 24.

35. *Nihon to Chūgoku no Aida*, p. 515.

36. *TYHS*, II, pp. 19–20.

37. *Nihon to Chūgoku no Aida*, p. 515.

38. Matsumoto, *op. cit.*, p. 190.

39. *TYHS*, III, pp. 24, ff.

40. Cf. Kuwabara Takeo's comments on Takeuchi in *Jōkyōteki*, p. 55; cf. also Kuwabara Takeo, "Takeuchi-san to Watakushi," *Tembō*, May 1977, pp. 26–30.

41. Cf. Lawrence Olson, "Intellectuals and 'the People': On Yoshimoto Takaaki," below.

42. *TYHS*, II, pp. 169, ff.

43. *Hōhō toshite no Ajia*, pp. 201–202.

44. *TYHS*, I, pp. 332, ff.

45. Nakasato Tatsuhiko, "Rojin Seishin to Jitsuzonshugi—Takeuchi Yoshimi no Shisō Hōhō ni tsuite," *Risō*, October 1954, pp. 84–98.

46. Ubukata Naokichi, "Rojin wo Ikasu Michi," *Chūgoku Kenkyū*, #10, January 1949, pp. 31–43. For further criticism of Takeuchi's understanding of democracy, cf. Umemoto Katsumi, Satō Noboru, Maruyama Masao, Gendai Nihon no Kakushin Shisō, Tokyo, Kawade Shobō Shinsha, 1966, pp. 38–39.

47. Yoshimoto Takaaki, "Sekaishi no naka no Ajia," *Chūō Kōron*, May 1979, pp. 145, ff.

48. For an account of this organization, cf. R. P. Dore, "The Tokyo Institute for the Science of Thought," *Far Eastern Quarterly*, XIII, November 1953, pp. 23–26. See below, chapter 4.

49. Tsurumi Shunsuke, *Tsurumi Shunsuke Chosakushū*, Tokyo, Chikuma Shobō, 1975, II, p. 321.

50. Takeuchi Yoshimi, *Jōkyōteki*, p. 21.

51. *Ibid.*

52. Yoshimoto Takaaki, "Jissenteki Mujun ni tsuite," *Bungei*, August 1966, pp. 219–220.

53. Kōsuge Shōzō, "Takeuchi Yoshimi Shi ni okeru Minzoku-shugi to Nihon Kyōsantō," *Bunka Hyōron*, June 1967, p. 31.

54. Yoshimoto Takaaki, "Jissenteki Mujun ni tsuite," p. 220.

55. *Ibid.*, pp. 220–221.

56. First published in *Kindai Nihon Shisōshi Kōza*, Tokyo, Chikuma Shobō, 1959, X. Reprinted in *TYHS*, III, 1966; reprinted again in *Kindai no Chōkoku*, Tokyo, Fūzambō, 1979, along with the original 1942 essays and transcription of the symposium concerning this subject. All references in this chapter to Takeuchi's essay are to this latter source.

57. Participants in the symposium included: Kobayashi Hideo, Kamei Katsuichirō, Hayashi Fusao, Miyoshi Tatsuharu, Nakamura Mitsuo, Kawakami Tetsutarō, (above members of Bungakukai); Suzuki Naritaka, Nishitani Keiji, Shimomura Toratarō, (above members of Kyoto University group); Moroi Saburō, Tsurura Hideo, Yoshimitsu Yoshihiko, Kikuchi Masashi.

58. *Kindai no Chōkoku*, 1979, pp. 5–271.

59. *Ibid.*, p. 294.

60. *Ibid.*, p. 284.

61. *Ibid.*, p. 306.

62. *Ibid.* On Justice Pal's judgement, cf. Richard Minear, *Victor's Justice*, Princeton, NJ, Princeton University Press, 1971, pp. 156–158.

63. Yoshimoto Takaaki, "Jōkyō e no Hatsugen—Takeuchi Yoshimi ni tsuite," *Shikō*, #50, June 30, 1978, p. 5.

64. *Ibid.* (To which Yoshimoto added: "If his thinking is Hegelian, that can't be helped.")

65. Takeuchi, *Fufukujū no Isan*, p. 34.

66. Tatsuma Shōsuke, *Takeuchi Yoshimi Chosaku Nōto*, Tokyo, Toshoshimbunsha, 1965, p. 142.

67. *Fufukujū no Isan*, pp. 90, ff.

68. *Ibid.*, pp. 96–97.

69. *Ibid.*, p. 155.

70. For the fullest English-language account, cf. George Packard, *Protest in Tokyo*, Princeton, NJ, Princeton University Press, 1966.

71. *Fufukujū no Isan*, p. 109.

72. *Ibid.*, p. 173.

73. *Ibid.*, p. 113.

74. *Ibid.*, p. 116.

75. *Ibid.*, p. 114.

76. *Ibid.*, p. 139.

77. *Ibid.*, p. 142.

78. *Ibid.*, p. 143.

79. *Ibid.*, p. 146.
80. Packard, *op. cit.*, p. 289.
81. *Fufukujū no Isan*, p. 150.
82. *Ibid.*, p. 187.
83. *Ibid.*, p. 197.
84. *Ibid.*, p. 198.
85. *Ibid.*, p. 229.
86. *Ibid.*
87. Takeuchi Yoshimi, *Tenkeiki*, Tokyo, Sōkisha, 1974, pp. 47–50. Cf. Kamachi, *op. cit.*
88. *Nihon to Chūgoku no Aida*, pp. 532–534.
89. *Jōkyōteki*, p. 80.
90. *Ibid.*, pp. 73–74.
91. *Tenkeiki*, pp. 22, ff.
92. Hidaka Rokurō, "Takeuchi Yoshimi no nokoshita Mono," *Tembō*, May 1977, pp. 30–35.
93. Tsurumi Shunsuke, "Chōji," *Tembō*, May 1977, p. 63.
94. Fujita Shōzō, "Takeuchi Yoshimi," *Tembō*, May 1977, p. 37.
95. Kuno Osamu, "Chōji," *Tembō*, May 1977, p. 57.
96. Oda Makoto, "Takeuchi Yoshimi no Ajia Ron ni tsuite," in *Sengo Bungaku to Ajia*, Tokyo, Mainichi Shimbunsha, 1978, pp. 214–264.
97. On an earlier generation's involvement in the Chinese revolution, cf. Marius Jansen, *The Japanese and Sun Yat-sen*, Cambridge, Mass., Harvard University Press, 1954.
98. Yoshimoto Takaaki, "Jissenteki Mujun ni tsuite," *Bungei*, August 1966, pp. 214–223.
99. Matsumoto, *op. cit.*, pp. 80–81.
100. Kuwabara Takeo, "Takeuchi-san to Watakushi," *Tembō*, May 1977, p. 28.
101. Cf. the reactions of Tsurumi Shunsuke in Takeuchi, *Jōkyōteki*, p. 178.
102. Yoshimoto Takaaki, "Sekaishi no naka no Ajia," *Chūō Kōron*, May 1979, pp. 138–150.
103. Interview with Etō Shinkichi, Tokyo, July 1979.
104. Interview with Takeuchi Teruko, Tokyo, July 9, 1979.
105. Interview with Nomura Kōichi, Tokyo, July 25, 1979.

CHAPTER 3

1. For "people" he used *taishū, minshū*, or occasionally *shomin*, hardly ever *kokumin* or *shimin* except pejoratively.

2. Cf. Katō Shūichi, "Nihon Bunka no Zasshusei," in *Nihon no Nai to Gai,* Tokyo, 1969, pp. 12–26.

3. Interview with Yoshimoto Takaaki, Tokyo, July 20, 1977. Taped excerpts of this interview appeared in *Gendai Shisō,* October 1977, pp. 28–47.

4. Nakamura Fumiaki, *Yoshimoto Takaaki Ron,* Tokyo, 1973, pp. 11–17, 58.

5. Yoshimoto Takaaki, *Zen Chosakushū,* Tokyo, Keisō Shobō, 1968, I, p. 107. Hereafter cited as *ZCS.*

6. Interview with Yoshimoto Takaaki, Tokyo, July 20, 1977.

7. Nakamura, *op. cit.,* pp. 166, ff.

8. *ZCS,* XV, p. 27.

9. Tsurumi Shunsuke, *Chosakushū,* Tokyo, 1975, II, pp. 228–229.

10. *Ibid.,* II, p. 230.

11. Nakamura, *op. cit.,* p. 262.

12. Quoted in *ibid.,* p. 35.

13. Interview with Yoshimoto Takaaki, Tokyo, July 20, 1977.

14. Tsurumi, *op. cit.,* II, p. 230.

15. *ZCS,* XV, p. 96.

16. *Ibid.,* XV, pp. 210–211.

17. *Ibid.,* XV, pp. 112–113.

18. *Ibid.,* XV, pp. 118–119.

19. *Ibid.,* XV, p. 157.

20. Yoshimoto Takaaki, *Geijutsuteki Teikō to Zasetsu,* Tokyo, 1963, pp. 24–26.

21. *Ibid.,* p. 86.

22. *Ibid.,* p. 70.

23. Cf., for example, "Love Song," in Thomas Fitzsimmons, tr., *Japanese Poetry Now,* New York, Schocken Books, 1972, pp. 49–50. For the Japanese version see Nakamura, *op. cit.,* p. 303.

24. *ZCS,* XII, p. 267.

25. Nakamura, *op. cit.,* pp. 229–230.

26. *Ibid.,* p. 233.

27. *ZCS,* XII, pp. 266–267.

28. *Ibid.,* XV, pp. 96–97.

29. Yoshimoto, *Geijutsuteki Teikō to Zasetsu,* pp. 95, 101.

30. *Ibid.,* p. 186.

31. *Ibid.,* p. 110.

32. This view was expressed by Prof. Maruyama Masao in an interview with the writer, Tokyo, July 21, 1977.

33. Shisō no Kagaku Kenkyūkai, ed., *Tenkō,* Tokyo, III, 1962, pp. 347–361. Cf. also Ōkuma Nobuyuki, "Yoshimoto Takaaki no Sensō Sekinin Ron," *Gendai Shi Techō,* VIII, 1972, p. 22.

34. Yoshimoto, *Geijutsuteki Teikō to Zasetsu,* p. 103. The note here is reminiscent of Rilke, one of Yoshimoto's youthful enthusiasms: cp. Rilke's "Who, if I cried, would hear me among the angelic orders?" *Duino Elegies,* tr. J. B. Leishman and Stephen Spender, New York, Norton, 1939, p. 21.

35. *Ibid.,* pp. 86–87.

36. Nakamura, *op. cit.,* p. 327.

37. Quoted in *ibid.,* p. 333.

38. Kobayashi Ikki, "Yoshimoto Takaaki no Kiseki to Dokusha," *Shiso no Kagaku,* #67, October 1976, p. 73.

39. *ZCS,* XIII, p. 33.

40. *Ibid.,* XIII, p. 42.

41. *Ibid.,* XIII, p. 44.

42. *Ibid.,* XIII, pp. 684–685. He would later be criticized for his lack of active support of *Beheiren,* the so-called "League for Peace in Vietnam." Cf. Yoshimoto Takaaki, *Doko ni Shisō no Konkyō o oku ka?,* Tokyo, 1972, pp. 205–206.

43. Shirakawa Masayoshi, *Yoshimoto Takaaki Ron,* Tokyo, 1971, p. 225.

44. *ZCS,* XIII, p. 56.

45. Nakamura, *op. cit.,* p. 342.

46. *ZCS,* XIII, p. 57.

47. *Ibid.,* XIII, pp. 60–61.

48. *Ibid.,* XIII, pp. 68–69.

49. *Ibid.,* XIII, pp. 84–86.

50. *Ibid.,* XIII, pp. 110–112.

51. *Ibid.,* XIII, p. 116.

52. *Ibid.,* XII, pp. 5–10, 12.

53. *Ibid.,* XII, p. 15.

54. *Ibid.,* XII, p. 55.

55. Maeda Ai, "Sengo ni okeru Dokusho no Hembō," *Shisō no Kagaku,* #67, October 1976, p. 6.

56. *ZCS,* XII, p. 67.

57. Maruyama Masao, *Studies in the Intellectual History of Tokugawa Japan,* Tokyo and Princeton, NJ, 1974, p. 29.

58. For recent evaluations of Maruyama's work, cf. Herman Ooms and H. D. Harootunian, "Maruyama's Achievement: Two Views," *Journal of Asian Studies,* XXXVI, 3, May 1977, pp. 521–

534; Tetsuo Najita, "Reconsidering Maruyama Masao's *Studies*," *The Japan Interpreter*, XI, 1, Spring 1976, pp. 97–108.

59. *ZCS*, XIII, p. 144.

60. *Ibid.*, XIII, p. 152.

61. *Ibid.*, XIII, pp. 208–210.

62. *Ibid.*, XIII, pp. 220, 228.

63. *Ibid.*, XIII, pp. 229–230.

64. *Ibid.*, XIII, p. 234.

65. Not all targets of his criticism accepted it in silence: Tsurumi Shunsuke thought Yoshimoto's feelings were too "pure," his writings almost religious in character and by implication fanatical. Cf. Yoshimoto, *Doko ni Shisō no Konkyō o oku ka?*, pp. 45, 49.

66. *ZCS*, XIII, p. 235. Italics in text.

67. *Ibid.*, XIII, pp. 238–239.

68. *Ibid.*, XIII, p. 266.

69. *Ibid.*, XIII, p. 262.

70. *Ibid.*

71. Maeda Ai, "Sengo ni okeru Dokusho no hembō," *Shisō no Kagaku*, #67, October 1976, p. 6.

72. *ZCS*, XIII, p. 273. These ideas about language were expanded upon in Yoshimoto's *Gengo ni totte Bi to wa Nani ka?*, Tokyo, Keisō Shobō, 1965.

73. *Ibid.*, XIII, pp. 316, ff.

74. *Ibid.*, XIII, p. 681. Professor Maruyama referred to Yoshimoto's "worshippers" (*sūhaisha*) and considered him the founder of a "new religion." Interview with Maruyama Masao, Tokyo, July 21, 1977.

75. Takayanagi Shin'ichi and Miwa Kimitada, eds., *Postwar Trends in Japan*, Tokyo, 1975, p. 218.

76. *Ibid.*, p. 219.

77. *Ibid.*

78. Ueyama Shumpei, *Nihon no Shisō, Dochaku to Ōka no Keifu*, Tokyo, 1971, p. 311.

79. *Ibid.*, pp. 318–320.

80. Interview with Yoshimoto Takaaki, Tokyo, July 20, 1977.

81. *Ibid.*

82. *Ibid.*

83. Interview with Maruyama Masao, Tokyo, July 21, 1977.

84. Takeuchi Yoshimi, *Hyōronshū*, Tokyo, Chikuma Shobō, 1966, II, pp. 30, ff. One critic complained that although Yoshimoto asked basic questions about man's plight, his image of man was too vague.

Cf. Tōmaru Ritsu, "Yoshimoto Takaaki Ron," *Chūō Kōron*, November 1968, pp. 272–278.

CHAPTER 4

1. Robert Scalapino, "Ideology and Modernization: the Japanese Case," in David E. Apter, ed., *Ideology and Discontent*, New York, The Free Press, 1964, p. 106. Italics in original.

2. Letter from Lawrence Terry to the author, May 10, 1984.

3. *Gendai Nihon Jimmei Jiten*, Tokyo, Hiebonsha, 1955, p. 461.

4. Tsurumi Shunsuke, *Tsurumi Shunsuke Chosakushū*, Tokyo, Chikuma Shobō, 1975, V, p. 370. Hereafter cited as *CSS*.

5. *Ibid.*

6. Tsurumi Shunsuke, *Watakushi no Chiheisen no ue ni*, Tokyo, Ushio Shuppansha, 1975, p. 26.

7. Data on Gotō Shimpei is from *Shinsen Dai Jimmei Jiten*, Tokyo, Heibonsha, 1982, pp. 624–625. See also Hayase Yukiko, *The Career of Gotō Shimpei: Japan's Statesman of Research*, unpublished doctoral dissertation, Florida State University, 1974.

8. *CSS*, V, pp. 367–368.

9. Letter from Tsurumi Shunsuke to the author, April 16, 1985.

10. *Ibid.*

11. *CSS*, V, p. 366.

12. *Ibid.*, pp. 366–367.

13. *Watakushi no Chiheisen no ue ni*, p. 73.

14. Tsurumi Shunsuke, *Futeikei no Shisō*, Tokyo, Bungei Shunjū, 1968, pp. 411–412.

15. *Ibid.*, p. 412.

16. *CSS*, V, p. 368.

17. *Watakushi no Chiheisen no ue ni*, p. 58.

18. Kan Takayuki, *Tsurumi Shunsuke Ron*, Tokyo, Dai San Bummeisha, 1980, p. 203.

19. S. Tsurumi, "Japanese Conceptions of Asia," Melbourne, Monash University Japanese Studies Center, 1982, p. 1. In English.

20. Except as otherwise noted, information about Tsurumi at Middlesex School is based upon files made available to the author by the school.

21. Tsurumi Shunsuke, *Ehagaki no Yohaku ni*, Tokyo, Tokyo Shoseki Kabushiki Kaisha, 1984, pp. 171–183.

22. Interview with Charles W. Young, Princeton, NJ, April 9, 1984.

23. Letter from Lawrence Terry to the author, May 10, 1984.

24. *Ibid.*

25. Tsurumi Shunsuke, *Hokubei Taiken Saikō,* Tokyo, Iwanami Shoten, 1971, p. 44.

26. Letter from Lawrence Terry to the author, May 10, 1984.

27. Interview with Charles W. Young, Princeton, NJ, April 9, 1984.

28. *Ehagaki no Yohaku ni,* p. 182.

29. Interview with Charles W. Young, Princeton, NJ, April 9, 1984. Cf. also Tsurumi Shunsuke, *Hon to Hito to,* Tokyo, Nishida Shoten, 1979, p. 12.

30. Charles W. Young recalled the strain in their relations after the attack on Pearl Harbor, when Tsurumi seemed to expect to be cast out but was not; Young maintains that his own warm feelings for Tsurumi survived the attack and never faltered. Interview with Charles W. Young, Princeton, NJ, April 9, 1984.

31. *Hon to hito to,* pp. 11–12.

32. *Hokubei Taiken Saikō,* p. 167.

33. *Ehagaki no Yohaku ni,* p. 185; *Hokubei Taiken Saikō,* p. 10.

34. For the fullest account of this period, cf. *Ehagaki no Yohaku ni,* pp. 185–193; see also *Futeikei no Shisō,* p. 73.

35. *Ehagaki no Yohaku ni,* p. 205.

36. *Ibid.*

37. *Ibid.,* p. 208.

38. *Watakushi no Chiheisen no ue ni,* p. 109.

39. *CSS,* I, p. 381; written in 1961.

40. *Hon to Hito to,* p. 13.

41. *Watakushi no Chiheisen no ue ni,* p. 115.

42. *Ehagaki no Yohaku ni,* p. 215.

43. *Ibid.,* p. 95.

44. *Ibid.,* p. 99.

45. *CSS,* I, p. 249.

46. *Ibid.,* I, pp. 353–383.

47. *Ibid.,* III, pp. 12–25.

48. *Ibid.,* I, p. 253.

49. *Ibid.,* I, pp. 13, 25.

50. *Ibid.,* I, pp. 38, ff.

51. *Ibid.,* I, pp. 68–69.

52. *Ibid.,* I, p. 75.

53. *Ibid.,* I, p. 178.

54. *Ibid.*

55. *Hokubei Taiken Saikō*, p. 168. One of his contemporaries was struck by the nostalgia *Amerika Tetsugaku* was capable of producing 25 years after its publication. See *CSS*, I, p. 5.

56. *Watakushi no Chiheisen no ue ni*, p. 158.

57. R. P. Dore, "The Tokyo Institute of the Science of Thought," *Far Eastern Quarterly*, XIII, 1, November 1953, p. 24.

58. Ōya Sōichi, *Ōya Sōichi Zenshū*, Tokyo, Sōyōsha, 1980–82, VI, p. 259.

59. Kan, *Tsurumi Shunsuke Ron*, p. 210.

60. Letter from Tsurumi Shunsuke to the author, August 8, 1984.

61. S. Tsurumi, "A Glimpse of Wartime Japan," Montreal, McGill University Center for East Asian Studies Occasional Paper #7, May 1980, p. 24. In English.

62. *CSS*, II, p. 7.

63. Letter from Tsurumi Shunsuke to the author, August 8, 1984.

64. *CSS*, II, pp. 64–89.

65. *Ibid.*, II, pp. 91–111.

66. *Kaitei Zōho Kyōdō Kenkyū: Tenkō*, Tokyo, Heibonsha, 1978, III, pp. 383–384. The revised edition of the original work. On Yoshimoto Takaaki, cf. *Yoshimoto Takaaki Zen Chosaku Shū*, Tokyo, Keisō Shobō, 1969, XV, pp. 5–27.

67. *Kaitei Zōho Kyōdō Kenkyū: Tenkō*, III, pp. 416–453.

68. *Ibid.*, III, p. 418.

69. *CSS*, II, p. 221.

70. *Ibid.*, II, pp. 254–255.

71. Tsurumi Shunsuke, *Amerika Shisō kara Nani wo Manabu ka?*, Tokyo, Chūō Kōronsha, 1958, p. 120.

72. *Ibid.*, p. 211.

73. *Gendai Nihon no Shisō*, Tokyo, Iwanami Shoten, 1956.

74. *Sengo Nihon no Shisō*, Tokyo, Keisō Shobō, 1959.

75. *CSS*, II, pp. 264–276.

76. Cf. George Packard, *Protest in Tokyo*, Princeton, NJ, Princeton University Press, 1966, pp. 275–276.

77. *Watakushi no Chiheisen no ue ni*, p. 164.

78. *CSS*, III, p. 209.

79. *Ibid.*, III, p. 218.

80. *Ibid.*, III, p. 210.

81. Katō Shūichi, *Katō Shūichi Chosakushū*, Tokyo, Heibonsha, 1979, VII, pp. 5–29.

82. *CSS*, III, p. 297.

83. *Ibid.*, III, pp. 271–272.

84. *Ibid.*, III, p. 298.
85. *Ibid.*, II, p. 203.
86. *Ibid.*, III, p. 395.
87. They continued to have this done until at least 1977. Cf. Kan, *op. cit.*, p. 207.
88. *CSS*, III, pp. 426, ff.
89. *Ibid.*, V, p. 89.
90. *Ibid.*, III, p. 439.
91. *Watakushi no Chiheisen no ue ni*, p. 80.
92. *CSS*, V, p. 100.
93. *Ibid.*, V, p. 101.
94. *Ibid.*, V, p. 122.
95. *Watakushi no Chiheisen no ue ni*, p. 80.
96. *Hokubei Taiken Saikō*, p. 20.
97. *Ibid.*, p. 88.
98. *Ibid.*, p. 167.
99. *Ibid.*, p. 60.
100. *Ibid.*, p. 121.
101. *Ibid.*, p. 164.
102. *Ibid.*, p. 168.
103. *Futeikei no Shisō*, p. 82.
104. Tsurumi Shunsuke, *Yanagi Muneyoshi*, Tokyo, Heibonsha, 1976, pp. 222–226.
105. Tsurumi Shunsuke, *Sengo Nihon no Taishū Bunka, 1945–1980*, Tokyo, Iwanami Shoten, 1984. Based on lectures delivered at McGill University, Montreal.
106. Tsurumi Shunsuke, *Senjiki Nihon no Seishin Shi*, Tokyo, Iwanami Shoten, 1982. Based on lectures given at McGill University, Montreal.
107. *Futeikei no Shisō*, p. 335.
108. *Watakushi no Chiheisen no ue ni*, p. 260.
109. *Futeikei no Shisō*, p. 338.

Index

173

Peirce, Charles Sanders, 113, 128–29
the people, 2, 10, 14, 29, 58, 66, 70, 74, 102, 105, 110, 114, 127–28, 132, 140, 144, 150; criticism of Takeuchi Yoshimi's views of, 60; defense of by Takeuchi Yoshimi, 58; Yoshimoto Takaaki and, 79–112
Perry, Ralph Barton, 121
Poe, Edgar Allan, 135
Police Duties Law, 67
policy science, 139
Potsdam Declaration, 34, 55
pragmatism, 104, 113, 121–22, 127, 128–30, 134, 138, 139, 143, 147
Princeton University, 2, 20–26
privatization, 95
propaganda, 90, 91, 128
protest, 15–16, 49, 53, 56–58, 66–69, 87–88, 90, 94, 95, 115, 132, 140–41, 144, 147

Rabbit Run, 22
rakugo, 138, 150
realism, 10, 10–11
realists, 87; Etō Jun's view on, 17–19; view of Etō Jun, 35–36
Recantation: A Cooperative Research Project, 133–38
Red Star Over China, 50
rentaikan, 54
revolution, 53, 58, 61, 69, 73, 89, 99, 132, 135; Chinese, 60, 64, 74
Rikkyō University, 144
Rimbaud, Arthur, 37, 135
Rojin (Lu Xun), 52–55
Romantic School, 62, 63
romanticism, 9, 19, 57–58, 81, 114
Russo-Japanese War, 24

Saga Rebellion of 1874, 4
Saigō Takamori, 40
Sakka wa Kōdō suru, 10–12, 14
San Francisco Peace Treaty, 3, 58
San Min Zhu I, 50
Sandburg, Carl, 81
Saroyan, William, 6
Sasebo naval base, 4
Satō Nobuhiro, 96
Scalapino, Robert, 114
Schlesinger, Arthur, Sr., 118
Schopenhauer, Arthur, 124
Second World War. *See* World War II
Security Treaty, 2, 40–41, 44, 67, 96, 103, 105, 149; Etō Jun, 15–17; Takeuchi Yoshimi and, 66–71, 75; Takeuchi Yoshimi's academic resignation and, 43–44; Tsurumi Shunsuke and, 140; Yoshimoto Takaaki and, 94–96
Seijuku to Sōshitsu, 26–29
seikatsu tsuzurikata undō, 139
sekai risei, 93
self-liberation, 8
senchūha, 83
Senkan Yamato no Saigo—Tengo Sakusen ni okeru Gunkan Yamato no Sentō Keika, 33
Sensei, 8
senzenha, 73
Shiga Naoya, 9
Shikō, 111
shimin, 110
shimin shakai, 7
Shimizu Ikutarō, 90, 134
Shimomura Tora-tarō, 64
shin, 76
Shinran, 107, 108
Shirakaba, 139
shiso, 18, 62, 104, 129, 130–31, 133–36, 138, 139
Shisō no Kagaku, 71, 131
shokuminchi bungaku, 7
Shōwa, 100
shūsai, 47, 76
shutaisei, 8, 13, 26, 28, 58, 86

About the Author

Lawrence Olson was born in Memphis, Tennessee in 1918 and was educated at the University of Mississippi and Harvard, where he took an M.A. in English literature in 1939 and a Ph.D. in Asian history and languages in 1955. During the Second World War he served in the U.S. Navy, graduating from the Navy Japanese Language School in Boulder, Colorado in 1943 and serving in the Pacific Fleet Radio Unit at Admiral Nimitz's headquarters in Pearl Harbor from 1943 until 1945.

Returning to civilian life in 1946, Mr. Olson found that his career interests had shifted to the newly defeated enemy, Japan. After holding several government positions, including that of the Cultural Attaché in the American Embassy in the Philippines, he returned to Harvard to complete his Ph.D. In 1955 he joined the American Universities Field Staff, Inc., a new non-profit organization devoted to providing in-depth studies of foreign societies through written reports and lectures in selected American universities. Between 1955 and 1966 Mr. Olson lived principally in Japan. In this period he wrote more than sixty studies on Japanese domestic developments and foreign relations. These were widely circulated among U.S. universities, government bureaus and other consumers, and established his reputation as a writer of clarity and an insightful observer of Japanese affairs. Out of this period came a book, *Dimensions of Japan* (1963).

During this period Mr. Olson also made four nationwide lecture tours, speaking to miscellaneous audiences and conducting student and faculty seminars at a dozen or more leading American universities. In 1970 he published *Japan in Postwar Asia* (Praeger), a study of Japan's changing relations with its Asian neighbors and a pioneer work on that subject. This book was sponsored by the Council on Foreign Relations, where Mr. Olson held a research fellowship. He also wrote a monograph on Japan for the Headline Series of the Foreign Policy Association, and an essay on U.S.-Japanese political relations in *The United States and Japan* (1965, reprinted 1975), a book edited by Herbert Passin and written for a meeting of the American Assembly.

In 1966 Mr. Olson assumed new duties as a professor of history at Wesleyan University, Middletown, Connecticut. There he was responsible for the creation and development of an East Asia Studies Program. In 1987 he was decorated by the Japanese government with the Order of the Sacred Treasure, Third Class, in recognition of his efforts over many years to widen the flow of accurate information about Japan to the American public.

In 1985 Mr. Olson moved in retirement to Washington, D.C., where he now lives.